The Merrill Studies
in
U.S.A.

Compiled by
David Sanders
Clarkson College of Technology

Charles E. Merrill Publishing Company
A Bell & Howell Company
Columbus, Ohio

CHARLES E. MERRILL STUDIES

Under the General Editorship of
Matthew J. Bruccoli and Joseph Katz

ISBN: 0-675-09154-3

Library of Congress Catalog Card Number: 76-180529

1 2 3 4 5 6 7 8–79 78 77 76 75 74 73 72

Printed in the United States of America

Preface

John Dos Passos wrote and published almost continuously from his graduation from Harvard in 1916 to his death in October, 1970. For ten of those fifty-four years, from 1927 to 1936, he worked on the novels which form *U.S.A.* The great trilogy is not his only significant achievement, but it does demonstrate more convincingly than anything else he wrote his restless experimentation with narrative technique and his preoccupation with the fates of individuals seeking to govern themselves.

Shortly after the executions of Nicola Sacco and Bartolomeo Vanzetti in 1927, Dos Passos began to write a novel which he hoped would account for whatever had happened in twentieth-century American history to bring about the deaths of the condemned anarchists. He did not then imagine a trilogy. "Course of Empire," "New Nation," and "New Era" are working titles written along the margins of his early typescripts. Before he had gotten very far with his project, it became clear to him that there were three sharply separate times in this history he was trying to shape into fiction. In the center of it all was the war. Before the war there had been a time of ironic aspirations. After the war came the harvest of wasted lives which other people would call the boom or the jazz age. So, the novel born of his anger outside Charlestown Prison became *The 42nd Parallel,* which describes the failure of an itinerant wobbly and the success of a public relations magnate amid scores of other real and fictional careers between the turn of the century and the time young Americans shipped overseas before "it all went bellyup." *1919* is about the war they set out to see and much more about the peace drawn at

iii

Versailles. Its central figure is "Meester Veelson," the wartime president for whom "the Word was God and God was the Word" in Dos Passos' merciless portrait. *The Big Money,* completing the trilogy, is about money so big that it displaces everything else. The fictional characters die or are worn out pursuing money; the historical figures are predominantly exploited inventors or such Veblenesque effigies of an acquisitive society as Rudolph Valentino and Samuel Insull.

This outline does not begin to suggest the richness or the excitement to be found in *U.S.A.* Nor can these qualities be conveyed by noting that each of the three novels is a montage of four elements: the narratives, the portraits or biographical sketches, the newsreels, and the autobiographical "Camera Eyes." The great distinction of *U.S.A.* rests, instead, on a twofold achievement much greater than the design of a "collectivist" or a "panoramic" novel. First, *U.S.A.* is a deeply personal book about the growth of an artist who begins life at a greater distance from the center of his subject than any of his other fictional or historical characters and who stands, at the end of *The Big Money,* in the eye of the revolutionary whirlwind outside the gates of Charlestown Prison singing *The Internationale.* It is this artist who cries, "all right, we are two nations." He remains alive and impassioned despite all the disgust and despair he records so thoroughly. Second, *U.S.A.* is unusually skillful satire. This is obvious enough in the biographies of politicians and capitalists or in the newsreels, which are crazy paste-ups of headlines, song lyrics, and fragments from news stories. It is somewhat subtler in the narratives. "*U.S.A.,*" Dos Passos wrote in his own headnote to the completed trilogy, "is the speech of the people." Each of his narratives perfectly illustrates this, for they are written in the precise speech of their subjects. If they could have seen themselves honestly and been capable of detached amusement, this is how J. Ward Moorehouse or Joe Williams or Eveline Hutchins would have described their lives. Instead, they are mouthpieces for Dos Passos' singular invention of a mocking omniscience.

The reviews and essays in this collection consider the individual novels as well as the completed trilogy. The most interesting contemporary notice of *The 42nd Parallel* appeared in a *New Republic* review by Edmund Wilson, entitled "Dahlberg, Dos Passos, and Wilder," which I have regretfully excluded because Mr. Wilson would not consent to its being reprinted out of the context in which he also wrote about *The Woman of Andros* and *The Bottom Dogs.* The reader is therefore directed to pages 446 to 450 of Mr. Wilson's *The Shores of Light.* Aside from this omission, the present collection comes close to representing the wide range of opinions about *U.S.A.* The reviews show how gravely it was received in the thirties and how difficult it was for some reviewers in 1936 and 1938 to reconcile Dos Passos' literary merit with the shifts they had discerned in his political thinking. (It would have been instructive to have added some of the reviews of his next novel, *Adventures of a Young Man,* published in 1939 just after the Spanish Civil War. Without exception they asserted that his disenchantment with the left had led to a decline in his writing, a view which held indiscriminately in most printed reactions to his work ever afterward.)

The only problem that arose in selecting the essays was that some of the best comments about *U.S.A.* have appeared in essays concerned about Dos Passos' politics or his self-definition as an observer. Any serious reader of Dos Passos should go on to those writings of Daniel Aaron, Richard Chase, Robert Gorham Davis, Martin Kallich, Kenneth Lynn, and Delmore Schwartz as well as another significant essay by Blanche Gelfant. Enough remains in the present compilation to suggest why *U.S.A.* is unlike anything else written by an American in this century and why Dos Passos meant as much as Ernest Hemingway or William Faulkner to a generation of college students now in their forties and fifties.

Surprisingly few full-length critical studies have been written about Dos Passos. John Wrenn's *John Dos Passos* (1961) is the best in English. *Themes et structures dans l'oeuvre de John Dos Passos* (1958), by Georges-Albert Astre, stops after two volumes with the critic's consideration of *The 42nd Parallel.* It is impossible to believe that other books will not appear soon.

I am grateful to Mrs. Alana Kahn and Mrs. Ruth Wood for their help in assembling these materials.

D.S.

Contents

1. Contemporary Reviews

2. Studies

1. Contemporary Reviews

Matthew Josephson

A Sad "Big Parade"

John Dos Passos has distinguished himself among contemporary novelists for ambition, resolution, and fecundity. Reading "1919" as a companion-piece to "The 42nd Parallel," as the second volume of a tetralogy—or is it to be perhaps an American "Comédie Humaine"?—one is enabled to glimpse much more of the hull of a huge literary cargo vessel, in the process of building, and to guess at the form of its upper decks and bridges. One tends to liken this series of historical novels, based upon the recent World War period, to Balzac's long work rather than to Zola's twenty-volume epic of "The Rougon-Macquarts" or to Thomas Mann's "Buddenbrooks," because both of the latter were confined to a single family, although Zola's, to be sure, was a family of a thousand members spreading into every corner of nineteenth century Europe. Proust, on the other hand, devoted himself solely to the upper class of French society.

The size of the author's framework, his social-historical objective, must be borne in mind if one would not be confused by the quick, episodic shifting of scenes and characters. The hero of "1919" is not a single person, but a great crowd, and more specifically a group of types out of the crowd. From one to another of these types the eye of the novelist moves back and forth: now he records the fictive biography of a "wobbly" in the American Northwest, now of a hypocrite, Harvard intellectual, now of a common, drifting sailor, or of a big publicity agent, or a middle-class Chicago flapper. These chronicles are systematically interlarded with a section of "newsreel," which is composed of a picturesque summation of newspaper headlines of the period; also with brief "biographies" of period characters, as likely to be of underground revolutionary fame, like John Reed or Wesley Everest, as of wider public note, like J. P. Morgan or "Meester Veelson." The style of the historical digression, a loose, dithyrambic, occasionally brilliant (through imagery) free verse, offers a marked contrast to that of the main narrative, soberly colloquial, behavioristic, almost monosyllabic. Besides lending some artistic relief, the digressions also serve as a sort of vivid backdrop against which the characters pass in procession. Yet the general reader should not be greatly disturbed by the impressionistic and experimental inter-

Reprinted from *The Saturday Review of Literature,* IX (March 19, 1932), 600, by permission of *Saturday Review.* ⓒ 1932 The Saturday Review Company, Inc.

ruptions; for each chapter of narrative is often a finished episode
in itself, or a character portrait in action. Sometimes, as in the long
opening chapter upon the sailor, Joe Williams, they form complete
and absorbing novelettes in themselves.

If we feared, in reading "The 42nd Parallel," that we were watching
too many disconnected characters and scenes falling apart, this fear
subsided before the increased effectiveness of "1919." We sense the
"collective" character of the various world-historical developments
which, driving the characters of the Dos Passos epic before them,
move toward the climax of the war's end.

The whole work is further unified by the author's consistent view
of the history he deals with: this, it is perhaps embarrassing to relate,
is nothing less than Marx's materialist conception of history as determined by the means of production. Indeed, the consistency of Dos
Passos is his shining distinction. Ever since the World War, it seems
to me, Dos Passos has stubbornly refused to believe either in the
benevolence of American capitalism or in the wonders of American
prosperity. Rather, he has been numbered among those who longed
to see the present order exchanged for that of a socialist and proletarian state. And although such principles may seem vexing to many
citizens who are perfectly aware that this is a free country, in which
everyone is free to find a job and save money, it is necessary to
touch upon them in passing so that the particular, grim color of
Dos Passos's novel may be better understood.

It is a matter of little surprise, then, that the account of Dos
Passos's troop of American characters in no way resembles a Horatio
Alger fable. Here in "1919" there are only driven beasts, eating,
drinking, fornicating, sliding always toward the line of least resistance.
This qualification goes for the types who represent learning or heavy
industry, as for the sailors, "wobblies," and up-to-date stenographers.
Many gently bred readers may possibly be forced to shut their eyes
and stop their noses at certain pages, since the novelist writes with
so much deliberate "bad taste." On the other hand, Earl Carroll and
a few movietones selected at random have left this reviewer wondering
what there is that the American public may still be shocked by.
The fecal is left—and Dos Passos does use this occasionally, like a
naughty boy, to rouse us or horrify us out of our indifference.

In any case, Dos Passos, energetic and impassioned novelist, is
leading the way—while groping at times—toward a proletarian literature; that is, a literature of revolution, something which certain of
our critics have been calling for. His novels strike one as being far
richer than those of the pedestrian Upton Sinclair (whom, however,

he has resembled enough in point of view upon America to have won a considerable European success). He is more imaginative than Dreiser, more intelligent than Sinclair Lewis, and exceeds both these able *tendenz* novelists in natural culture. Dos Passos is little more than thirty-five; has written a dozen volumes of prose fiction and drama, and is improving in power. He has his pronounced limitations, over which, one hopes, his courage and will may prevail.

One may well quarrel with his style, for one thing. In the direct narrative of "1919" there is, plainly enough, a systematic avoidance of all rhetorical elegance, adherence only to bare, factual chronicle of outward movements, which admits of no "inwardness" in the characters. In this behavioristic manner certain of our modern neo-realists believe they approach their subject more closely than ever before, and without the intervention of sentiment. Yet it cannot be denied that such a method gives at times a monotonous and unlovely texture to the literary monolith which Dos Passos is building, however respectable his motives may be. Besides, he contradicts these motives in his digressive interludes which are done, as I have pointed out, in a picturesque and impressionistic free verse. On the whole, Dos Passos's innovations of language (ugly neologisms) and of style (a heedless colloquialism introduced into the text, a pell-mell syntax), seem neither appetizing nor important. Tolstoy wrote epic novels designed for universal reading without holding himself to a nearly monosyllabic vocabulary; Zola, save for the instance of one early novel, wrote a tolerably pure French; and both of them have been read by millions of proletarians.

One still has the feeling, finally, that Dos Passos portrays types rather than characters, though he does seem to work out the destiny of each type within the logical limits of heredity and background. One could wish that he had Hemingway's shrewd eye for character and the special accidents thereof, with which a bullfighter is pictured as so thoroughly a bullfighter. Yet if Dos Passos had such an eye, perhaps he would not have so remarkable a bird's-eye view for the collective and panoramic drama which he evokes in "1919."

Malcolm Cowley

The End of a Trilogy

Most of the characters in "The Big Money" had been introduced to us in the two earlier novels of the series. Charley Anderson, for example, the wild Swedish boy from the Red River Valley, had first appeared at the end of "The 42nd Parallel," where we saw him drifting over the country from job to job and girl friend to girl friend, then sailing for France as the automobile mechanic of an ambulance section. Now he comes sailing back as a bemedaled aviator, hero and ace. He helps to start an airplane manufacturing company (like Eddie Rickenbacker); he marries a banker's daughter, plunges in the stock market, drinks, loses his grip and gets killed in an automobile accident. Dick Savage, the Harvard esthete of doubtful sex, had appeared in "1919" as an ambulance driver. Now he is an advertising man, first lieutenant of the famous J. Ward Moorehouse in his campaign to popularize patent medicines as an expression of the American spirit, as self-reliance in medication. Eveline Hutchins, who played a small part in both the earlier novels, is now an unhappy middle-aged nymphomaniac. Don Stevens, the radical newspaper man, has become a Communist, a member of the Central Executive Committee after the dissenters have been expelled (and among them poor Ben Compton, who served ten years in Atlanta for fighting the draft). New people also appear: for example, Margo Dowling, a shanty-Irish girl who gets to be a movie actress by sleeping with the right people. Almost all the characters are now tied together by love or business, politics or pure hatred. And except for Mary French, a Colorado girl who half-kills herself working as the secretary of one radical relief organization after another—except for Mary French and poor honest Joe Askew, they have let themselves be caught in the race for easy money and tangible power; they have lost their personal values; they are like empty ships with their seams leaking, ready to go down in the first storm.

Read by itself, as most people will read it, "The Big Money" is the best of Dos Passos' novels, the sharpest and swiftest, the most unified in mood and story. Nobody has to refer to the earlier books in order to understand what is happening in this one. But after turning back to "The 42nd Parallel" and "1919," one feels a new admiration for Dos Passos as an architect of plots and an interweaver

From *The New Republic*, LXXXVIII (August 12, 1936), 23-24. Copyright 1936 by Editorial Publications, Inc. Reprinted by permission of the author.

of destinies. One learns much more about his problems and the original methods by which he has tried to solve them.

His central problem, of course, was that of writing a collective novel (defined simply as a novel without an individual hero, a novel of which the real protagonist is a social group). In this case the social group is almost the largest possible: it is the United States from the Spanish War to the crash of 1929, a whole nation during thirty years of its history. But a novelist is not a historian dealing with political tendencies or a sociologist reckoning statistical averages. If he undertakes to depict the national life, he has to do so in terms of individual lives, without slighting either one or the other. This double focus, on the social group and on the individual, explains the technical devices that Dos Passos has used in the course of his trilogy.

It is clear enough that each of these devices has been invented with the purpose of gaining a definite effect, of supplying a quality absent from the narrative passages that form the body of the book. Take the Newsreels as an example of these technical inventions. The narratives have dealt, necessarily, with shortsighted people pursuing their personal aims—and therefore the author intersperses them with passages consisting of newspaper headlines and snatches from popular songs, his purpose being to suggest the general or collective atmosphere of a given period. Or take the brief biographies of prominent Americans. The narrative sections have dealt with people like Charley Anderson and Dick Savage, fairly typical Americans, figures that might have been chosen from a crowd—and therefore the author also gives us life-sketches of Americans who were representative rather than typical, the leaders or rebels of their age.

The third of Dos Passos' technical devices, the Camera Eye, is something of a puzzle and one that I was a long time in solving to my own satisfaction. Obviously the Camera Eye passages are autobiographical, and obviously they are intended to represent the author's stream of consciousness (a fact that explains the lack of capitalization and punctuation). At first it seemed to me that they were completely out of tone with the hard and behavioristic style of the main narrative. But this must have been exactly the reason why Dos Passos introduced them. The hard, simple, behavioristic treatment of the characters has been tending to oversimplify them, to make it seem that they were being approached from the outside— and the author tries to counterbalance this weakness by inserting passages that are written from the inside, passages full of color and warmth and hesitation and little intimate perceptions.

I have heard Dos Passos violently attacked on the ground that all these devices—Newsreels and biographies and the Camera Eye—were presented arbitrarily, without relation to the rest of the novel. This attack is partly justified as regards "The 42nd Parallel," though even in that first novel there is a clearer interrelation than most critics have noted. For instance, the Camera Eye describes the boyhood of a well-to-do lawyer's son and thereby points an artistically desirable contrast with the boyhood of tough little Fainy McCreary. Or again, the biography of Big Bill Haywood is inserted at the moment in the story when Fainy is leaving to help the Wobblies win their strike at Goldfield. Many other examples could be given. But when we come to "1919," connections of this sort are so frequent and obvious that even a careless reader could not miss them; and in "The Big Money" all the technical devices are used to enforce the same mood and the same leading ideas.

Just what are these ideas that Dos Passos is trying to present? . . . The question sounds more portentous than it is in reality. If novels could be reduced each to a single thesis, there would be no reason for writing novels: a few convincing short essays would be all we needed. Obviously any novelist is trying to picture life as it is or was or as he would like it to be. But his ideas are important in so far as they help him to organize the picture (not to mention the important question of their effect on the reader).

In Dos Passos' case, the leading idea is the one implicit in his choice of subject and form: it is the idea that life is collective, that individuals are neither heroes nor villains, that their destiny is controlled by the drift of society as a whole. But in what direction does he believe that American society is drifting? This question is more difficult to answer, and the author doesn't give us much direct help. Still, a certain drift or progress or decline can be deduced from the novel as a whole. At the beginning of "The 42nd Parallel" there was a general feeling of hope and restlessness and let's-take-a-chance. A journeyman printer like Fainy McCreary could wander almost anywhere and find a job. A goatish but not unlikable fraud like old Doc Bingham could dream of building a fortune and, what is more, could build it. But at the end of "The Big Money," all this has changed. Competitive capitalism has been transformed into monopoly capitalism; American society has become crystalized and stratified. "Vag"—the nameless young man described in the last three pages of the novel—is waiting at the edge of a concrete highway, his feet aching in broken shoes, his belly tight with hunger. Over his head flies a silver transcontinental plane filled with highly paid executives on their way to the Pacific Coast. The upper class has taken to the air, the lower class to the road; there is no longer any bond between them; they are two nations. And we ourselves, if we choose the side of the defeated nation, are reduced to being foreigners in the land where we were born.

That, I suppose, is the author's thesis, if we reduce it to a bald statement. Dos Passos prefers to keep it in the background, suggesting it time and again. The tone of his last volume is less argumentative than emotional—and indeed, we are likely to remember it as a furious and somber poem, written in a mood of revulsion even more powerful than that which T. S. Eliot expressed in "The Waste Land." Dos Passos loves the old America; he loathes the frozen country that the capitalists have been creating—and when he describes it he makes it seem like an inferno in which Americans true to the older spirit are crushed and broken. But for the hired soldiers of the conquering nation—for J. Ward Moorehouse and Eleanor Stoddard and Dick Savage and all their kind—he reserves an even sharper torture: to be hollow and enameled, to chirp in thin squeaky voices like insects with the pulp of life sucked out of them and nothing but thin poison left in their veins. Rich, empty, frantic, they preside over an icy hell from which Dos Passos sees no hope of our ever escaping.

Anonymous

Private Historian

Old history is in books and new on front pages. Yet neither tells the whole story of a people, a period, a place. Behind the extraordinary news in the papers, the decisive events described by historians, lies a mass of anonymous, miscellaneous human happenings, comprising the routine stuff of daily living. This is private history, and, though it rarely gets into public history, it outweighs soldiers and statesmen, battles and booms, in the final balance of time.

Reprinted by permission from TIME, The Weekly Newsmagazine, XXVIII (August 10, 1936), 51-52. Copyright Time Inc., 1936.

To relate these minutiae of contemporary experience to the broad sweep of historical developments has been the task for the past ten years of a novelist named John Roderigo Dos Passos. Last week Author Dos Passos, 40, offered readers a novel called *The Big Money* that stood midway between history and fiction, the last of a series of three books that constitute a private, unofficial history of the U. S. from 1900 to 1929.

The Method. With *The Big Money* John Dos Passos brought to a close one of the most ambitious projects that any U. S. novelist has undertaken. *The 42nd Parallel, 1919,* and *The Big Money* run to 1449 pages, detail the careers of some 13 major characters and a host of minor ones, picture such widely separated locales as pre-War Harvard, Wartime Paris, Miami during the Florida boom, Hollywood, Greenwich Village, Detroit. This trilogy also includes 27 brief biographies of such representative public figures as Steinmetz, Luther Burbank, Henry Ford, Sam Insull, Hearst, Isadora Duncan, Rudolph Valentino, artfully spaced throughout the three volumes. The author provides, in addition, a shorthand autobiography in the form of 51 poetic interludes called *The Camera Eye,* which show his own attitude toward the events in which his characters are involved. Like most works of fiction that are written in tandem, each novel in Dos Passos' series makes sense in its own right, gains in cumulative intensity if read in its place in the whole impressive scheme.

Appearing complicated to the point of bewilderment at first glance, this narrative method emerges in *The Big Money* as ingeniously simple. Basis of the book is the life stories of a few men and women whose careers converge or parallel each other. Some, like the promising but spineless Harvard intellectual Dick Savage, have figured prominently in the previous volumes. Red-faced, hard-drinking Charley Anderson barely appeared in *The 42nd Parallel.* Margo Dowling, dissolute and disillusioned cinema queen makes her debut in *The Big Money.* Dos Passos' method is to follow one of his characters through some meaningful experience or period in his life, then shift to another. Between chapters he inserts the short biography of some real public figure whose career forms an oblique commentary on the imaginary character just described.

Charley Anderson, for example, is a well-meaning, good-hearted aviator who won the *Croix de guerre* in the War. He has genuine mechanical ability, works as a mechanic for a time, gets along well with plain men when he sees them as individuals. But pursuit of the Big Money corrupts his native talents as well as his good nature, eventually kills him. Dos Passos frames the story of Anderson with thumbnail sketches of Henry Ford, Frederick Winslow Taylor, inventor of scientific management, and Thorstein Veblen. Like Ford, Charley Anderson had native mechanical skill, loved to tinker with machines. Like Taylor, he suffered because he tried to speed up production, to make manufacture efficient, and shrank from the resulting hostility of workmen. Veblen, a lifelong student of the conflict between production and finance, who saw the constant "sabotage of production by business," adds an ironic footnote to Charley's tragedy.

Thus Dos Possos intimates that the stories of his characters are not exceptional or unique, that the waste, confusion, purposelessness in their lives, as well as their good human qualities and inborn talents, also appear in the lives of famed figures in public history.

The Material. The Big Money begins with the return of Charley Anderson from France. After a brief glimpse of Manhattan, he gets a cramped job as mechanic in his brother's garage in St. Paul. But Charley wants to get in on aviation's ground floor, incidentally pick up some of the Big Money he sniffs in the post-War air. Almost as soon as he gets it, women and liquor finish him off.

Mary French takes a different road. A Colorado doctor's daughter who hates her hateful mother, she goes from Vassar into settlement work and from there into the labor movement, falls in love with one radical hero after another, only to be betrayed by all of them. Drowning her personal despair in work for the Cause, she finally emerges as an impersonal, efficient cog in Revolution's painfully assembling machine.

Margo Dowling, on the other side of the fence, starts as a child actress, survives a nearly disastrous marriage to a Cuban pervert to become successively show girl, mistress, Hollywood extra and at last a queen of the screen.

Richard Ellsworth Savage, first introduced in *1919* as a young Harvard poet turned opportunist among the glittering opportunities of the Peace Conference, is shown in *The Big Money* as a prematurely tired junior executive who works hard at being yes-man to J. Ward Moorehouse, the great stuffed shirt of the public relations world. When J. Ward finally falters, Dick Savage is right there to take over.

Besides these principal pegs on which Author Dos Passos hangs his narrative, scores of other characters appear, reappear and fade away. Eveline Hutchins, the Chicago Jazz-age girl, attains a Manhattan salon only to end her career with an overdose of sleeping powder. G. H. Barrow, labor-faker, gets a paunch and a fur overcoat by "settling" strikes. Ben Compton, a Brooklyn Jew turned radical and one of Mary French's lovers, finds his life ruined when he is read out of the Party for being a "disrupting influence." All of them—in politics, manufacturing, advertising, Wall Street, the cinema—are swimming for their lives in the stream of the Big Money, fighting desperately against the current, sucked under or bobbing successfully along with the descending river.

The Manner. Two unique fictional devices, in addition to the biographies of famed individuals, interrupt the stories of these people in their rapid rises and catastrophic falls. One is the *Newsreel,* an effective muddle of headlines, fragments of speeches, new stories, popular songs. Each about a page long, they serve to fix the time of the action as well as to suggest the general moral and intellectual climate of the U. S. during the period. Thus the *Newsreel* that follows a chapter telling of Margo Dowling's miserable marriage includes a song that was popular at the moment, headline reference to topics that were then being discussed:

> . . . *the kind of a girl that men forget*
> *Just a toy to enjoy for a while*
> Coolidge Pictures Nation Prosperous Under His Politics
> > PIGWOMAN SAW SLAYING
> > Saw a Woman Resembling Mrs. Hall Berating
> > Couple Near Murder Scene, New Witness Says
> > SHEIK SINKING
> Rudolph Valentino, noted screen star, collapsed suddenly yesterday in his apartment at the Hotel Ambassador. Several hours later he underwent. . . .

Last and most perplexing of Dos Passos' innovations is *The Camera Eye.* Purpose of these autobiographical prose poems is to suggest the shifting point of view of the author as he turns his imagination on the characters who fill his book and the combination of influences that have made him the individual he is and given him the point of view he holds. Like fragmentary warnings scattered through the volumes, they constantly remind the reader of the author's bias, warn him that Dos Passos' picture of reality has been colored by his personal experiences. After the chapter in *The Big Money* describing Charley Anderson's return to the U. S., *The Camera Eye* relates memories of Dos Passos' own homesick return after the War:

> *spine stiffens with the remembered chill of the off shore Atlantic*
>
> *and the jag of framehouses in the west above the invisible land and spiderweb rollercoasters and the chewinggum towers of Coney and the freighters with their stacks way aft and the blur beyond Sandy Hook.*

Then the ordeal of looking for a job in the post-War Depression:

> *the pastyfaced young man wearing somebody else's readymade busi-*
> *ness opportunity*
> *is most assuredly not*
> *the holder of any of the positions for which he made application*
> *at the employment agency*

By the time readers have followed the careers of Dos Passos' characters, studied the sharp, ironic sketches of U. S. public heroes, absorbed the confusion and hysteria of the *Newsreels,* they are likely to feel that they have received a vivid cross-section report on some U. S. history in a manner neither novelists nor historians supply. They may question whether ordinary private life during that period was as confused and chaotic as Dos Passos represents it, whether he has not overshot his mark in bringing so many of his characters to violent ends, so many of their hopes to tragic frustrations. But they can admire without reservation his narrative style, bare but not bleak, naturalistic but not dull, and his cunning blend of the literary and the colloquial. Dos Passos believes that a writer's modest job is to be an "architect of history." He never talks about creation in connection with his work. His job, he feels, is simply to arrange the materials, confining any artistic high jinks to decoration that will enhance the outlines of the building without weakening its structure.

Granville Hicks

The Moods and Tenses
of John Dos Passos

John Dos Passos' publishers are wisely doing their part to make the country conscious of him as a major literary figure, and they have accordingly issued two omnibus volumes of his work. *U.S.A.*

Reprinted from *New Masses,* XXVII (April 26, 1938), 22-23, by permission of New Outlook Publishers and the author.

is, of course, his famous trilogy: *The 42nd Parallel, 1919,* and *The Big Money. Journeys Between Wars* is made up of his travel books: much of *Rosinante to the Road Again* (1922), almost the whole of *Orient Express* (1927) and most of those sections of *In All Countries* (1934) that deal with foreign lands. It also contains some sixty pages on Dos Passos' visit to Spain a year ago.

Comparison of the two books makes it quite clear that Dos Passos' deeper experiences go into his novels leaving his more casual impressions to be recorded in the travel essays. *Journeys Between Wars* shows he is at his best when he is describing the persons he meets or recording his moods. The padrone in the Spanish restaurant, the Sayid on the Orient Express, the Danish accountant on his way home from America—these are effectively drawn. And the journal of the camel ride from Bagdad to Damascus is as pleasant a personal record as can be found in modern literature. But there is not much—and I have read most of these essays twice—that the mind holds on to. Other novelists—Gide, Lawrence, Huxley—have written travel books that belong in their major works, but not Dos Passos.

The explanation which has some importance for the understanding of Dos Passos as a writer seems to me fairly clear. He deals, consistently and no doubt deliberately, with impressions—the specific scene, the precise emotions, the exact conversation. The seeing eye—even the "camera eye"—is admittedly the first virtue of the travel writer. But it is equally certain that the memorable travel writers have not been afraid to draw conclusions from what they saw. Dos Passos is afraid: no milder word will do. What one feels in *Journeys Between Wars* is neither a casual holiday from the job of thinking nor a conscientious elimination of ideas for some literary purpose, but a deep emotional unwillingness to face intellectual implications of things seen and heard.

And the extraordinary thing is that this shrinking from conclusions is to be found even in the last section, the section dealing with Spain in 1937. Dos Passos tells of crossing the border from France, of a night on the road, of executions in Valencia, of a bombardment of Madrid, of a fiesta of the Fifteenth Brigade, of a trip through some villages, and of an interview with officials of the POUM. But there is not a word about the issues between the loyalists and the fascists, not a word about the differences between the loyalist government and the POUM. It seems incredible that any author, considering all that is involved in Spain today, could keep such silence. Do not suppose that Dos Passos is merely maintaining an artistic objectivity, holding back his own opinions so that the reader can arrive unhampered at the truth. He simply has refused to think his way through to clear convictions. He has sympathies—with the loyalists as against the fascists and apparently with the POUM as against the government. But even the Spanish crisis cannot shake him into thought.

The only approximation to a conclusion comes as Dos Passos is leaving Spain, and characteristically, it is in the form of a question: "How can they win, I was thinking? How can the new world of confusion and cross purposes and illusion and dazzled by the mirage of idealistic phrases win against the iron combination of men accustomed to run things who have only one idea binding them together, to hold on to what they've got?" This passage has been quoted by almost every conservative reviewer of the book, and quoted with undisguised satisfaction. "We told you so," one could hear them saying. "There's no sense in trying to help Spain. It's all foolishness to hope for social justice anywhere. Let's make the best of things as they are."

The truth is that it is impossible to avoid having opinions, and the only question is whether or not they are based on adequate information and clear thinking. If Dos Passos had faced the responsibility of the writer, and especially the radical writer to use his intellect as well as his eyes, if he had been concerned, not with avoiding conclusions but with arriving at sound ones, I think he would have come out of Spain with something more to say than these faltering words of despair. Afraid to think, he has yielded to a mood, and the reactionaries are delighted with his surrender. Both that surrender and his flirtation with the POUM are the results of an essential irresponsibility.

Dos Passos' irresponsibility takes two forms: unwillingness to think and unwillingness to act. Several years ago, I remember, at the time when he was perhaps closest to the Communist party, he said something to the effect that he was merely a camp-follower. In *Journeys Between Wars* there is a revealing passage (It is, of course, creditably characteristic of Dos Passos to reveal himself). When he was leaving the Soviet Union in 1928, the director and actors of the Sanitary Propaganda Theater came to see him off. The director said, "They want to know. They like you very much, but they want to ask you one question. They want you to show your face. They want to know where you stand politically. Are you with us?" Dos Passos continues: "The iron twilight dims, the steam swirls around us, we are muddled by the delicate crinkly steam of our breath, the iron crown tightens on the head, throbbing with too many men, too many women, too many youngsters seen, talked to, asked questions of, too many hands shaken, too many foreign languages badly understood. 'But let me see . . . But maybe I can explain . . . But in so short a time . . . there's not time.' The train is moving. I have to run and jump for it."

The passage, so palpably sincere and so pleasant, reminds us that, even in a broader sense, Dos Passos has always been uncommonly detached. Indeed, detachment is almost the keynote of *Journeys Between Wars*. In the extracts from *Rosinante,* Dos Passos is "the traveller", in Orient Express, he is "the east-bound American"; in the Russian section, he is the "Amerikanski peesatyel." Perhaps it is no wonder that in writing about 1937 he is still merely an observer. It is no wonder that he has seldom tried to write about the revolutionary movement from the inside, and when he has tried, he has failed. It is no wonder that he has never communicated the sense of the reality of comradeship, as Malraux, for example, communicates it in *Days of Wrath.*

Yet there was a time when Dos Passos seemed willing to try to think clearly and feel deeply. His second play, *Airways, Inc.,* was bad dramatically, but in it Dos Passos at least made an attempt to be clear. There was a sharp difference between that play and *The Garbage Man* and an even greater difference between *The 42nd Parallel,* first novel of his trilogy, and *Manhattan Transfer.* In *The 42nd Parallel,* Dos Passos seemed for the first time to have mastered the American scene. The technical devices used in this novel and *1919* perplexed some readers, but Dos Passos himself appeared to be relatively clear about what he was trying to do.

Airways, Inc. was published in 1928, *The 42nd Parallel* in 1930, and *1919* in 1932. Here, then, are three or four years of comparative clarity. And in those years Dos Passos was close to Communism. At this time he actually believed in something like the Marxian analysis of history, and it worked. He also felt a stronger confidence in the working class. Communism did not make him a novelist, but it made him a better novelist.

What I failed to realize at the time of the publication of *1919* was the extent to which Dos Passos' interest in the Communist movement was a matter of mood. He had not sufficiently overcome his fear of conclusions to make a serious study of Marxism and he had only partly subdued his passion for aloofness. Little things could—and as it happened did—disturb him. He was on the right track, but not much was required to derail him.

In the four years since he has left the track, Dos Passos has gone a long and disastrous way. Last summer, as has been said, he came out of Spain with nothing but a question mark, and committed himself to a hysterical isolationism that might almost be called chauvinistic. Last December he and Theodore Dreiser held a conversation that was published in *Direction.* Dos Passos' confusion—equalled I hasten to say, by Dreiser's—is unpleasant to contemplate for anyone who expects some semblance of intellectual dignity in a prominent novelist. He is still looking for an impartial observer of the Soviet Union, and thinks he has found one in Victor Serge. His new-found devotion to the United States continues to run high: "America is probably the country where the average guy has got a better break." "You can't get anywhere," he says, "in talking to fanatic Communists." He talks about revolution: "A sensible government would take over industries and compensate the present owners and then deflate the money afterwards." And this is his contribution to economics: "Every time there is a rise in wages, prices go up at the A & P."

After one has noted the banality, the naivete, and the sheer stupidity of most of Dos Passos' remarks in his talk with Dreiser, one knows that politically he is as unreliable as a man can be and is capable of any kind of preposterous vagary. But I am interested in Dos Passos' politics only insofar as they influence his writings, as of course they do. When *1919* appeared, I believed that Dos Passos had established his position as the most talented of American novelists—a position he still holds. As early as 1934, however, I was distressed by his failure to shake off habits of mind that I had thought, quite erroneously it turns out, were dissolving under the influence of contact with the revolutionary movement. At the time, reviewing *In All Countries,* I said: "Dos Passos, I believe, is superior to his bourgeois background because he is, however incompletely, a revolutionist, and shares, however imperfectly, in the vigor of the revolutionary movement, its sense of purpose, its awareness of the meaning of events, and its defiance of bourgeois pessimism and decay. He is also, it seems to me, superior to any other revolutionary writer because of the sensitiveness and the related qualities that are to be found in this book and much more abundantly in his novels. Some day, however, we shall have a writer who surpasses Dos Passos, who has all that he has and more. He will not be a camp follower."

Now that Dos Passos is not in any sense a revolutionist and does not share at all in the vigor of the revolutionary movement, what about the virtues that I attributed to his association with the Communist party? I am afraid the answer is in *The Big Money,* most of which was written after 1934. One figure dominates *The Big Money* to an extent that no one figure dominated either *The 42nd Parallel* or *1919*. It is Charley Anderson, the symbol of the easy-money Twenties, the working stiff who gets to be a big shot. ("America is probably the only country where the average guy has got a better break.") His desperate money-making and drinking and fornicating take place against a background of unhappy rich people and their unhappy parasites. Further in the background are some equally unhappy revolutionists who are either futile or vicious. ("You can't get anywhere with talking to fanatic Communists.")

It seems to me foolish to pretend that an author doesn't choose his material. Dos Passos didn't have to lay his principal emphasis on the hopeless mess that the Capitalist system makes of a good many lives. He didn't have to make his two Communists narrow sectarians. He didn't have to make the strongest personal note in the book a futilitarian elegy for Sacco and Vanzetti. There must have been a good deal in the Twenties that he left out, for large masses of people did learn something from the collapse of the boom, and the Communist party did get rid of factionalism, and the workers did save Angelo Herndon and the Scottsboro Boys, even though they failed to save Sacco and Vanzetti. *The Big Money,* in other words, grows out of the same prejudices and misconceptions, and the same confusion and blindness, as the conversation with Dreiser.

The difference is, of course, that there is a lot in *The Big Money* besides these faulty notions. I have written elsewhere about Dos Passos' gifts and I need only say here that I admire them as strongly as ever. I know of no contemporary American work of fiction to set beside *U.S.A.* But I also know that, because of the change in mood that came between *1919* and *The Big Money, U.S.A.* is not so true, not so comprehensive, not so strong as it might have been. And though I have acquired caution enough not to predict Dos Passos' future direction, I know that, if he follows the path he is now on, his claims to greatness are already laid before us, and later critics will only have to fill in the details of another story of a genius half-fulfilled.

T. K. Whipple

Dos Passos and the U. S. A.

The choice of the ambitious title "U.S.A." for the volume which brings together Dos Passos's "The 42nd Parallel," "Nine-teen-Nineteen," and "The Big Money" looks as if it might be intended to stake out a claim on the fabulous "great American novel." And Dos Passos's claim is not a weak one. A single book could hardly be more inclusive than his: in the stories of his main characters he covers most parts of the country during the first three decades of the twentieth century. His people have considerable social diversity, ranging from Mac, the I.W.W. typesetter, and Joe Williams, the feckless sailor, to Ben Compton, the radical leader, Eleanor Stoddard, the successful decorator, Margo Dowling, the movie star, and J. Ward Moorehouse, the big publicity man. The background of the panorama is filled out with "newsreels" of newspaper headlines, popular songs, and the like, with the autobiographic "camera eye" which gives snatches of Dos Passos's own experience, and with a series of bio-graphical portraits of representative men—Debs, Edison, Wilson, Joe Hill, Ford, Veblen, Hearst, and twenty more. Probably no other American novel affords a picture so varied and so comprehensive.

Furthermore, the picture is rendered with extraordinary vividness and brilliance of detail, especially of sensory detail. Sights and sounds and above all smells abound until the reader is forced to wonder that so many people of such different sorts, are all so constantly aware of what their eyes and ears and noses report to them: might not some of them, one asks, more often get absorbed in meditation or memory or planning or reverie? But it is no part of Dos Passos's scheme to spend much time inside his characters' heads; he tells, for the most part, what an outsider would have seen or heard—ges-tures, actions, talk, as well as the surroundings. The result is a tribute to the keenness of the author's observation—not only of colors, noises, and odors but, even more important, of human behavior and of American speech. People as well as things are sharp and distinct.

Reprinted from *The Nation,* CXLVI (February 19, 1938), 210-12, by permission of Mrs. Mary Ann Whipple.

Nor does the presentation lack point and significance. As the book goes on, the U.S.A. develops, with the precision of a vast and masterly photograph, into a picture of a business world in its final ripeness, ready to fall into decay. Though Dos Passos does not call himself a Marxist—and would seem in fact not to be one—his point of view is unmistakably radical. The class struggle is present as a minor theme; the major theme is the vitiation and degradation of character in such a civilization. Those who prostitute themselves and succeed are most completely corrupted; the less hard and less self-centered are baffled and beaten; those who might have made good workers are wasted; the radicals experience internal as well as external defeat. No one attains any real satisfaction. Disintegration and frustration are everywhere. The whole presentation leads to the summary: "Life is a shambles." Perhaps there are implications that it need not be; but no doubt is left that actually it is.

These generalities, when stated as generalities, have of course become the trite commonplaces of a whole school of literature. But actual people shown going through the process of victimization can never become trite or commonplace; the spectacle must always be pitiful and terrible. And no one, I should suppose, could look on Dos Passos's picture wholly untouched and unmoved. But still one might ask whether he has quite achieved the tragic effect which presumably he aimed at.

To complain that the picture is one-sided may appear captious and unreasonable, and in one sense of "one-sided" it is. The whole truth about a hundred million people throughout thirty years cannot be told in fifteen hundred—or in fifteen million—pages. The novelist has to select what he considers representative and characteristic persons and events, and if Dos Passos has chosen to omit big business men, farmers, and factory workers, and to dwell chiefly on midway people in somewhat ambiguous positions—intellectuals, decorators, advertising men—perhaps that is his privilege. The question is whether this picture of his which is surely extensive enough as novels go, is entirely satisfactory within the limitations which must be granted. How close does "U.S.A." come to being a great American novel? That it comes within hailing distance is proved by the fact that it has already been so hailed; indeed, it comes close enough so that the burden of proof is on those who would deny the title. Yet to grant it offhand would be premature.

On one point at least everyone probably agrees: that the biographical portraits are magnificent, and are the best part of the book. But wherein are they superior? Is it not that these portraits have a greater depth and solidity than Dos Passos's fictional characterizations—a more complete humanity? If so, the implication must be that his creation of character is not complete. And indeed when Mac is put beside Big Bill Haywood, or Ben Compton beside Joe Hill and Jack Reed, or Margo Dowling beside Isadora Duncan, the contrast is unflattering to Dos Passos's powers as a novelist. There is more human reality in the 10 pages given to Henry Ford than in the 220 given to Charley Anderson. Nor is the explanation that the real people are exceptional, the fictitious ones ordinary, satisfactory: some of the fictitious ones are supposed to be leaders; and besides it is a novelist's business so to choose and treat his imagined characters as to reveal his themes in their utmost extension, not at their flattest. No; the contrast has nothing to do with the positions people occupy; it is a fundamental matter of the conception of human nature and the portrayal of it in literature.

In thinking of this contrast, one notices first that the real men have a far better time of it in the world, that they do find a good many genuine satisfactions, that even when they fail—when they are jailed like Debs or shot down like Joe Hill—they are not wholly defeated. Inside them is some motive power which keeps them going to the end. Some of them swim with the stream and some against it, but they all swim; they all put up a fight. They all have persistent ruling passions. Furthermore, they are all complex and many-sided, full of contradictions and tensions and conflicts. They have minds, consciousness, individuality, and personality.

Not that all these things are entirely lacking in the fictitious characters—Dos Passos is too good a novelist for that—but they do appear only in a much lower degree, played down, degraded, reduced to a minimum. As a result, the consciousness of these people is of a relatively low order. True, they are aware with an abnormal keenness of their sensations, but is not this sensory awareness the most elementary form of consciousness? On the other hand, these folk can hardly be said to think at all, and their feelings are rather sharp transitory reactions than long-continuing dominant emotions. Above all, they are devoid of will or purpose, helplessly impelled hither and yon by the circumstances of the moment. They have no strength of resistance. They are weak at the very core of personality, the power to choose. Now it may be that freedom of choice is an illusion, but if so it is an inescapable one, and even the most deterministic and behavioristic novelist cannot omit it or minimize it without denaturing human beings. When the mainspring of choice is weakened or left out, the conflicts and contradictions of character lose their virtue and significance, and personality almost disappears. Dos Passos often gives this effect: that in his people there is, so to speak, nobody much at home, or that he is holding out on us and that more must be happening than he is willing to let on. This deficiency shows itself most plainly in the personal relations of his characters—they are hardly persons enough to sustain real relations with one another, any more than billiard balls do—and in his treatment of crisis, which he is apt to dispose of in some such way as: "They had a row so that night he took the train . . . "

The final effect is one of banality—that human beings and human life are banal. Perhaps this is the effect Dos Passos aimed at, but that it is needless and even false is proved by the biographical portraits, in which neither the men nor their lives are ever banal. The same objection holds, therefore, to Dos Passos's whole social picture as to his treatment of individuals, that he has minimized something vital and something which ought to be made much of—namely, forces in conflict. Society is hardly just rotting away and drifting apart; the destructive forces are tremendously powerful and well organized, and so are the creative ones. Furthermore, they are inextricably intermingled in institutions and in individuals. If Dos Passos is forced, by sheer fact, to present them so when he writes of Ford and Steinmetz and Morgan, why should he make little of them in his fiction? Is it to illustrate a preconceived and misleading notion that life nowadays is a silly and futile "shambles"?

One might hope, but in vain, to find the answer in the autobiographic "camera eye." To be sure, the author there appears as the extremest type of Dos Passos character, amazingly sensitive to impressions, and so amazingly devoid of anything else that most of the "camera eye" is uninteresting in the extreme. The effect of this self-portrait is further heightened by the brief prologue which introduces "U.S.A.": an account of a young man, plainly the author himself, who "walks by himself searching through the crowd with greedy eyes, greedy ears taut to hear, by himself, alone," longing to share everybody's life, finding his only link with other people in listening to their talk. If the obvious conclusion could be accepted that Dos Passos had been never a participant but always a mere onlooker hungry for participation, so that he had to depend only on observation from outside, it would explain much. But such is not the fact; he took part in the World War and in the Sacco-Vanzetti case and other activities. He has been no mere spectator of the world. Moreover, he must have had powerful and lasting purposes and emotions to have written his books, and it is hardly credible that he has done so little thinking as he makes out. His self-portrait must be heinously incomplete, if only because he is a real man. But it is possible that he may have chosen to suppress some things in himself and in his writing, and that he may have acquired a distrust of thought and feeling and will which has forced him back upon sensations as the only reliable part of experience. Some such process seems to have taken place in many writers contemporary with him, resulting in a kind of spiritual drought, and in a fear lest they betray themselves or be betrayed by life. Perhaps the disillusionment of the war had something to do with it, but more probably a partial view and experience of our present society are responsible.

According to any view, that society, in all conscience, is grim enough, but not banal, not undramatic. Dos Passos has reduced what ought to be a tale of full-bodied conflicts to an epic of disintegration and frustration. That reduction—*any* reduction—is open to objection, because it is an imperfect account of human beings and human society that does not present forces working in opposition. In that sense "U.S.A." is one-sided, whereas life and good literature are two-sided or many-sided. In a word, what we want is a dialectic treatment of people and the world. Dos Passos does not call himself a Marxist; if he were more of one, he might have written a better novel. The biographical portraits are the best part of his book because they are the most nearly Marxist, showing the dynamic contradictions of our time in the only way they can be shown—namely, as they occur in the minds and lives of whole men. Nothing will do, in the end, but the whole man.

Lionel Trilling

The America of John Dos Passos

U.S.A. is far more impressive than even its three impressive parts—*42nd Parallel, 1919, The Big Money*—might have led one to expect. It stands as the important American novel of the decade, on the whole more satisfying than anything else we have. It lacks

Reprinted from *Partisan Review* IV (April, 1938), 26-32, by permission of *Partisan Review* and the author. © 1938 by *Partisan Review*.

any touch of eccentricity; it is startlingly normal; at the risk of seeming paradoxical one might say that it is exciting because of its quality of cliché: here are comprised the judgments about modern American life that many of us have been living on for years.

Yet too much must not be claimed for this book. To-day we are inclined to make literature too important, to estimate the writer's function at an impossibly high rate, to believe that he can encompass and resolve all the contradictions, and to demand that he should. We forget that, by reason of his human nature, he is likely to win the intense perception of a single truth at the cost of a relative blindness to other truths. We expect a single man to give us all the answers and produce the "synthesis." And then when the writer, hailed for giving us much, is discovered to have given us less than everything, we turn from him in a reaction of disappointment: he has given us nothing. A great deal has been claimed for Dos Passos and it is important, now that *U.S.A.* is completed, to mark off the boundaries of its enterprise and see what it does not do so that we may know what it does do.

One thing *U.S.A.* does not do is originate; it confirms but does not advance and it summarizes but does not suggest. There is no accent or tone of feeling that one is tempted to make one's own and carry further in one's own way. No writer, I think, will go to school to Dos Passos, and readers, however much they may admire him will not stand in the relation to him in which they stand, say, to Stendhal or Henry James or even E. M. Forster. Dos Passos' plan is greater than its result in feeling; his book *tells* more than it *is*. Yet what it tells, and tells with accuracy, subtlety and skill, is enormously important and no one else has yet told it half so well.

Nor is *U.S.A.* as all-embracing as its admirers claim. True, Dos Passos not only represents a great national scene but he embodies, as I have said, the cultural tradition of the intellectual Left. But he does not encompass—does not pretend to encompass in this book— all of either. Despite his title, he is consciously selective of his America and he is, as I shall try to show, consciously corrective of the cultural tradition from which he stems.

Briefly and crudely, this cultural tradition may be said to consist of the following beliefs, which are not so much formulations of theory or principles of action as they are emotional tendencies: that the collective aspects of life may be distinguished from the individual aspects; that the collective aspects are basically important and are good; that the individual aspects are, or should be, of small interest and that they contain a destructive principle; that the fate of the individual is determined by social forces; that the social forces now dominant are evil; that there is a conflict between the dominant social forces and other, better, rising forces; that it is certain or very likely that the rising forces will overcome the now dominant ones. *U.S.A.* conforms to some but not to all of these assumptions. The lack of any protagonists in the trilogy, the equal attention given to many people, have generally been taken to represent Dos Passos' recognition of the importance of the collective idea. The book's historical apparatus indicates the author's belief in social determination. And there can be no slightest doubt of Dos Passos' attitude to the dominant forces of our time: he hates them.

But Dos Passos modifies the tradition in three important respects. Despite the collective elements of his trilogy, he puts a peculiar importance upon the individual. Again, he avoids propounding any sharp conflict between the dominant forces of evil and the rising forces of good; more specifically, he does not write of a class struggle, nor is he much concerned with the notion of class in the political sense. Finally, he is not at all assured of the eventual triumph of good; he pins no faith on any force or party—indeed he is almost alone of the novelists of the Left (Silone is the only other one that comes to mind) in saying that the creeds and idealisms of the Left may bring corruption quite as well as the greeds and cynicisms of the established order; he has refused to cry "Allons! the road lies before us," and, in short, his novel issues in despair.—And it is this despair of Dos Passos' book which has made his two ablest critics, Malcolm Cowley and T. K. Whipple, seriously temper their admiration. Mr. Cowley says: "They [the novels comprising *U.S.A.*] give us an extraordinarily diversified picture of contemporary life, but they fail to include at least one side of it—the will to struggle ahead, the comradeship in struggle, the consciousness of new men and new forces continually rising." And Mr. Whipple: "Dos Passos has reduced what ought to be a tale of full-bodied conflicts to an epic of disintegration."

These critics are saying that Dos Passos has not truly observed the political situation. Whether he has or not, whether his despair is objectively justifiable, cannot, with the best political will in the world, be settled on paper. We hope he has seen incorrectly; he himself must hope so. But there is also an implicit meaning in the objections which, if the writers themselves did not intend it, many readers will derive, and if not from Mr. Whipple and Mr. Cowley then from the book itself: that the emotion in which *U.S.A.* issues is negative to the point of being politically harmful.

But to discover a political negativism in the despair of *U.S.A.* is to subscribe to a naive conception of human emotion and of the literary experience. It is to assert that the despair of a literary work must inevitably engender despair in the reader. Actually, of course, it need do nothing of the sort. To rework the old Aristotlean insight, it may bring about a catharsis of an already existing despair. But more important the word "despair" all by itself (or any other such general word or phrase) can never characterize the emotion the artist is dealing with. There are many kinds of despair and what is really important is what goes along with the general emotion denoted by the word. Despair with its wits about it is very different from despair that is stupid; despair that is an abandonment of illusion is very different from despair which generates tender new cynicisms. The "heartbreak" of *Heartbreak House,* for example, is the beginning of new courage and I can think of no more useful *political* job for the literary man today than, by the representation of despair, to cauterize the exposed soft tissue of too-easy hope.

Even more than the despair, what has disturbed the radical admirers of Dos Passos' work is his appearance of indifference to the idea of the class struggle. Mr. Whipple correctly points out that the characters of *U.S.A.* are all "midway people in somewhat ambiguous positions." Thus, there are no bankers or industrialists (except incidentally) but only J. Ward Morehouse, their servant; there are no factory workers (except, again, incidentally), no farmers, but only itinerant workers, individualistic mechanics, actresses, interior decorators.

This, surely, is a limitation in a book that has had claimed for it a complete national picture. But when we say limitation we may mean just that or we may mean falsification, and I do not think that Dos Passos has falsified. The idea of class is not simple but complex. Socially it is extremely difficult to determine. It cannot be determined, for instance, by asking individuals to what class they belong; nor is it easy to convince them that they belong to one class or another. We may, to be sure, demonstrate the idea of class at income-extremes or function-extremes, but when we leave these we must fall back upon the criterion of "interest"—by which we must mean *real* interest ("real will" in the Rousseauian sense) and not what people say or think they want. Even the criterion of action will not determine completely the class to which people belong. Class, then, is a useful but often undetermined category of political and social thought. The political leader and the political theorist will make use of it in ways different from those of the novelist. For the former the important thing is people's perception that they are of one class or another and their resultant action. For the latter the interesting and suggestive things are likely to be the moral paradoxes that result from the conflict between real and apparent interest. And the "midway people" of Dos Passos represent this moral-paradoxical aspect of class. They are a great fact in American life. It is they who show the symptoms of cultural change. Their movement from social group to social group—from class to class, if you will—makes for the uncertainty of their moral codes, their confusion, their indecision. Almost more than the people of fixed class, they are at the mercy of the social stream because their interests cannot be clear to them and give them direction. If Dos Passos has omitted the class struggle, as Mr. Whipple and Mr. Cowley complain, it is only the external class struggle he has left out; within his characters the class struggle is going on constantly.

This, perhaps, is another way of saying that Dos Passos is primarily concerned with morality, with personal morality. The national, collective, social elements of his trilogy should be seen not as a bid for completeness but rather as a great setting, brilliantly delineated, for his moral interest. In his novels, as in actual life, "conditions" supply the opportunity for personal moral action. But if Dos Passos is a social historian, as he is so frequently said to be, he is that in order to be a more complete moralist. It is of the greatest significance that for him the barometer of social breakdown is not suffering through economic deprivation but always moral degeneration through moral choice.

This must be said in the face of Mr. Whipple's description of Dos Passos' people as "devoid of will or purpose, helplessly impelled hither and yon by the circumstances of the moment. They have no strength of resistance. They are weak at the very core of personality, the power to choose." These, it would seem, are scarcely the characters with which the moralist can best work. But here we must judge not only by the moral equipment of the characters (and it is not at all certain that Mr. Whipple's description is correct: choice of action is seldom made as the result of Socratic dialectic) but by the novelist's idea of morality—the nature of his judgments and his estimate of the power of circumstance.

Dos Passos' morality is concerned not so much with the utility of an action as with the quality of the person who performs it. *What* his people do is not so important as *how* they do it, or what they become by doing it. We despise J. Ward Morehouse not so much for his creation of the labor-relations board, his support of the war, his advertising of patent-medicines, though these are despicable enough; we despise him rather for the words he uses as he does these things, for his self-deception, the tone and style he generates. We despise G. H. Barrow, the labor-faker, not because he betrays labor; we despise him because he is mealy-mouthed and talks about "the art of living" when he means concupiscence. But we do not despise the palpable fraud, Doc Bingham, because, though he lies to everyone else, he does not lie to himself.

The moral assumption on which Dos Passos seems to work was expressed by John Dewey some thirty years ago; there are certain moral situations, Dewey says, where we cannot decide between the ends; we are forced to make our moral choice in terms of our preference for one kind of character or another: "What sort of an agent of a person shall he be? This is the question finally at stake in any genuinely moral situation: What shall the agent *be?* What sort of character shall he assume? On its face, the question is what he shall *do,* shall he act for this or that end. But the incompatibility of the ends forces the issue back into the questions of the kind of selfhood of agency, involved in the respective ends." One can imagine that this method of moral decision does not have meaning for all times and cultures. Although dilemmas exist in every age, we do not find Antigone settling her struggle between family and state by a reference to the kind of character she wants to be, nor Orestes settling his in that way; and so with the medieval dilemma of wife vs. friend, or the family oath of vengeance vs. the feudal oath of allegiance. But for our age with its intense self-consciousness and its uncertain moral codes, the reference to the quality of personality does have meaning and the greater the social flux the more frequent will be the interest in qualities of character rather than in the rightness of the end.

The modern novel, with its devices for investigating the quality of character, is the aesthetic form almost specifically called forth to exercise this modern way of judgment. The novelist goes where the law cannot go; he tells the truth where the formulations of even the subtlest ethical theorist cannot. He turns the moral values inside out to question the worth of the deed by looking not at its actual outcome but at its tone and style. He is subversive of dominant morality and under his influence we learn to praise what dominant morality condemns; he reminds us that benevolence may be aggression, that the highest idealism may corrupt. Finally, he gives us the models of the examples by which, half-consciously, we make our own moral selves.

Dos Passos does not primarily concern himself with the burly sinners who inherit the earth. His people are those who sin against themselves and for him the wages of sin is death—of the spirit. The whole Dos Passos morality and the typical Dos Passos fate are in Burns' quatrain:

> *I waive the quantum o' the sin,*
> *The hazard of concealing;*
> *But, och! it hardens a' within*
> *And petrifies the feeling!*

In the trilogy physical death sometimes follows upon this petrifaction of the feeling but only as its completion. Only two people die without petrifying, Joe Williams and Daughter, who kept in their inarticulate way a spark of innocence, generosity and protest. Idealism does not prevent the consequences of sinning against oneself and Mary French with her devotion to the working class and the Communist Party, with her courage and "sacrifice" is quite as dead as Richard Savage who inherits Wardhouse's [sic] mantle, and she is almost as much to blame.

It is this element of blame, of responsibility, that exempts Dos Passos from Malcolm Cowley's charge of being in some part committed to the morality of what Cowley calls the Art Novel—the story of the Poet and the World, the Poet always sensitive and right, the World always crass and wrong. An important element of Dos Passos' moral conception is that, although the World does sin against his characters, the characters themselves are very often as wrong as the world. There is no need to enter the theological purlieus to estimate how much responsibility Dos Passos puts upon them and whether this is the right amount. Clearly, however, he holds people like Savage, Fainy McCreary and Eveline Hutchins accountable in some important part of their own fates and their own ignobility.

The morality of Dos Passos, then, is a romantic morality. Perhaps this is calling it a bad name; people say they have got tired of a morality concerned with individuals "saving" themselves and "realizing" themselves. Conceivably only Dos Passos' aggressive contemporaneity has kept them from seeing how very similar is his morality to, say, Browning's—the moment to be snatched, the crucial choice to be made, and if it is made on the wrong (the safe) side, the loss of human quality, so that instead of a man we have a Success and instead of two lovers a Statue and a Bust in the public square. But too insistent a cry against the importance of the individual quality is a sick cry—as sick as the cry of "Something to live for" as a

motivation of political choice. Among members of a party the considerations of solidarity, discipline and expedience are claimed to replace
all others and moral judgment is left to history; among liberals, the
idea of social determination, on no good ground, appears tacitly to
exclude the moral concern: witness the nearly complete conspiracy
of silence or misinterpretation that greeted Silone's *Bread and Wine,*
which said not a great deal more than that personal and moral—and
eventually political—problems were not settled by membership in a
revolutionary party. It is not at all certain that it is political wisdom
to ignore what so much concerns the novelist. In the long run is
not the political choice fundamentally a choice of personal quality?

2. Studies

John Dos Passos and "1919"

A novel is a mirror. So everyone says. But what is meant by *reading* a novel? It means, I think, jumping into the mirror. You suddenly find yourself on the other side of the glass, among people and objects that have a familiar look. We have never really seen them. The things of our world have, in turn, become outside reflections. You close the book, step over the edge of the mirror and return to this honest-to-goodness world, and you find furniture, gardens and people who have nothing to say to you. The mirror that closed behind you reflects them peacefully, and now you would swear that art is a reflection. There are clever people who go so far as to talk of distorting mirrors.

Dos Passos very consciously uses this absurd and insistent illusion to impel us to revolt. He had done everything possible to make his novel seem a mere reflection. He has even donned the garb of populism. The reason is that his art is not gratuitous; he wants to prove something. But observe what a curious aim he has. He wants to show us this world, our own—to *show* it only, without explanations or comment. There are no revelations about the machinations of the police, the imperialism of the oil kings or the Ku-Klux-Klan, no cruel pictures of poverty. We have already seen everything he wants to show us, and, so it seems at first glance, seen it exactly as he wants us to see it. We recognize immediately the sad abundance of these untragic lives. They are our own lives, these innumerable, planned, botched, immediately forgotten and constantly renewed adventures that slip by without leaving a trace, without involving anyone, until the time when one of them, no different from any of the others, suddenly, as if through some clumsy trickery, sickens a man for good and throws a mechanism out of gear.

Now, it is by depicting, as we ourselves might depict, these too familiar appearances with which we all put up that Dos Passos makes them unbearable. He arouses indignation in people who never get indignant, he frightens people who fear nothing. But hasn't there been some sleight-of-hand? I look about me and see people, cities, boats, the war. But they aren't the real thing; they are discreetly queer and sinister as in a nightmare. My indignation against this world also seems dubious to me; it only faintly resembles the other

Reprinted by permission of The Philosophical Library, Inc. from *Literary Essays* by Jean-Paul Sartre (New York: Philosophical Library, 1957), pp. 88-96, © Copyright, 1955, by The Philosophical Library, Inc., New York.

indignation, the kind that a mere news item can arouse. I am on the other side of the mirror.

Dos Passos' hate, despair and lofty contempt are real. But that is precisely why his world is not real; it is a created object. I know of none—not even Faulkner's or Kafka's—in which the art is greater or better hidden. I know of none that is more precious, more touching or closer to us. This is because he takes his material from our world. And yet, there is no stranger or more distant world. Dos Passos has invented only one thing, an art of story-telling. But that is enough to create a universe.

We live in time, we calculate in time. The novel, like life, unfolds in the present. The perfect tense exists on the surface only; it must be interpreted as a present *with aesthetic distance,* as a stage device. In the novel the dice are not loaded, for fictional man is free. He develops before our eyes; our impatience, our ignorance, our expectancy are the same as the hero's. The tale, on the other hand, as Fernandez has shown, develops in the past. But the tale explains. Chronological order, life's order, barely conceals the causal order, which is an order for the understanding. The event does not touch us; it stands half-way between fact and law. Dos Passos' time is his own creation; it is neither fictional nor narrative. It is rather, if you like, historical time. The perfect and imperfect tenses are not used simply to observe the rules; the reality of Joe's or of Eveline's adventures lies in the fact they are now part of the past. Everything is told as if by someone who is remembering.

> 'The years Dick was little he never heard anything about his Dad . . . ' 'All Eveline thought about *that winter* was going to the Art Institute . . . ' 'They waited two weeks in Vigo while the officials quarrelled about their status and they got pretty fed up with it.'

The fictional event is a nameless presence; there is nothing one can say about it, for it develops. We may be shown two men combing a city for their mistresses, but we are not told that they "do not find them," for this is not true. So long as there remains one street, one cafe, one house to explore, it is not yet true. In Dos Passos, the things that happen are named first, and then the dice are cast, as they are in our memories.

> Glen and Joe only got ashore for a few hours and couldn't find Marcelline and Loulou.

The facts are clearly outlined; they are ready for *thinking about.* But Dos Passos never thinks them. Not for an instant does the order of causality betray itself in chronological order. There is no narrative, but rather the jerky unreeling of a rough and uneven memory, which sums up a period of several years in a few words only to dwell languidly over a minute fact. Like our real memories, it is a jumble of miniatures and frescoes. There is relief enough, but it is cunningly scattered at random. One step further would give us the famous idiot's monologue in *The Sound and the Fury*. But that would still involve intellectualizing, suggesting an explanation in terms of the irrational, suggesting a Freudian order beneath this disorder. Dos Passos stops just in time. As a result of this, past things retain a flavour of the present; they still remain, in their exile, what they once were, inexplicable tumults of colour, sound and passion. Each event is irreducible, a gleaming and solitary *thing* that does not flow from anything else, but suddenly arises to join other things. For Dos Passos, narrating means adding. This accounts for the slack air of his style. "And . . . and . . . and . . . " The great disturbing phenomena—war, love, political movements, strikes—fade and crumble into an infinity of little odds and ends which can just about be set side by side. Here is the armistice:

> In early November rumours of an armistice began to fly around and then suddenly one afternoon Major Wood ran into the office that Eleanor and Eveline shared and dragged them both away from their desks and kissed them both and shouted, "At last it's come." Before she knew it Eveline found herself kissing Major Moorehouse right on the mouth. The Red Cross office turned into a college dormitory the night of a football victory: It was the Armistice.
>
> Everybody seemed suddenly to have bottles of cognac and to be singing, *There's a long long trail awinding* or *La Made-lon pour nous n'est pas sevère*.

These Americans see war the way Fabrizio saw the battle of Waterloo. And the intention, like the method, is clear upon reflection. But you must close the book and reflect.

Passions and gestures are also things. Proust analysed them, related them to former states and thereby made them inevitable. Dos Passos wants to retain only their factual nature. All he is allowed to say is, "In that place and at that time Richard was that way, and at another time, he was different." Love and decisions are great spheres that rotate on their own axes. The most we can grasp is a kind of *conformity* between the psychological state and the exterior situation, something resembling a colour harmony. We may also suspect that explanations are *possible,* but they seem as frivolous and futile as a spider-web on a heavy red flower. Yet, never do we have the feelings of fictional freedom: Dos Passos imposes upon us instead the unpleasant impression of an indeterminacy of detail. Acts, emotions and ideas suddenly settle within a character, make themselves at home and then disappear without his having much to say in the matter. You cannot say he submits to them. He experiences them. There seems to be no law governing their appearance.

Nevertheless, they once did exist. This lawless past is irremediable. Dos Passos has purposely chosen the perspective of history to tell a story. He wants to make us feel that the stakes are down. In *Man's Hope,* Malraux says, more or less, that "the tragic thing about death is that it transforms life into a destiny". With the opening lines of his book, Dos Passos settles down into death. The lives he tells about are all closed in on themselves. They resemble those Bergsonian memories which, after the body's death, float about, lifeless and full of odours and lights and cries, through some forgotten limbo. We constantly have the feeling that these vague, human lives are destinies. Our own past is not at all like this. There is not one of our acts whose meaning and value we cannot still transform even now. But beneath the violent colours of these beautiful, motley objects that Dos Passos presents there is something petrified. Their significance is fixed. Close your eyes and try to remember your own life, try to remember it *that way;* you will stifle. It is this unrelieved stifling that Dos Passos wanted to express. In capitalist society, men do not have lives, they have only destinies. He never says this, but he makes it felt throughout. He expresses it discreetly, cautiously, until we feel like smashing our destinies. We have become rebels; he has achieved his purpose.

We are rebels *behind the looking-glass.* For that is not what the rebel of this world wants to change. He wants to transform Man's *present* condition, the one that develops day by day. Using the past tense to tell about the present means using a device, creating a strange and beautiful world, as frozen as one of those Mardi-Gras masks that become frightening on the faces of real, living men.

But whose memories are these that unfold through the novel? At first glance, they seem to be those of the heroes, of Joe, Dick, Fillette and Eveline. And, on occasion, they are. As a rule, whenever a character is sincere, whenever he is bursting with something, no matter how, or with what:

When he went off duty he'd walk home achingly tired through the strawberry-scented early Parisian morning, thinking of the faces and the eyes and the sweat-drenched hair and the clenched fingers clotted with blood and dirt . . .

But the narrator often ceases to coincide completely with the hero. The hero could not quite have said what he does say, but you feel a discreet complicity between them. The narrator relates from the outside what the hero would have wanted him to relate. By means of this complicity, Dos Passos, without warning us, has us make the transition he was after. We suddenly find ourselves inside a horrible memory whose every recollection makes us uneasy, a bewildering memory that is no longer that of either the characters or the author. It seems like a chorus that remembers, a sententious chorus that is accessory to the deed.

> All the same he got along very well at school and the teachers liked him, particularly Miss Teazle, the English teacher, because he had nice manners and said little things that weren't fresh but that made them laugh. Miss Teazle said he showed real feeling for English composition. One Christmas he sent her a little rhyme he made up about the Christ Child and the three Kings and she declared he had a gift.

The narration takes on a slightly stilted manner, and everything that is reported about the hero assumes the solemn quality of a public announcement:" . . . she declared he had a gift". The sentence is not accompanied by any comment, but acquires a sort of collective resonance. It is a *declaration*. And indeed, whenever we want to know his characters' thoughts, Dos Passos, with respectful objectivity, generally gives us their declarations.

> Fred . . . said the last night before they left he was going to tear loose. When they got to the front he might get killed and then what? Dick said he liked talking to the girls but that the whole business was too commercial and turned his stomach. Ed Schuyler, who'd been nicknamed Frenchie and was getting very continental in his ways, said that the street girls were too naive.

I open *Paris-Soir* and read, *"From our special correspondent: Charlie Chaplin declares that he has put an end to Charlie."* Now I have it! Dos Passos reports all his characters' utterances to us in the style of a statement to the Press. Their words are thereby cut off from thought, and become pure utterances, simple reactions that must be registered as such, in the behaviourist style upon which Dos Passos draws when it suits him to do so. But, at the same time, the Utterance takes on a social importance; it is inviolable, it becomes a maxim. Little does it matter, thinks the satisfied chorus, what Dick had in mind when he spoke that sentence. What matters is that it has been uttered. Besides, it was not formed inside him, it came from afar. Even before he uttered it, it existed as a pompous sound, a taboo. All he has done is to lend it his power of affirmation. It is as if there were a Platonic heaven of words and commonplaces to which we all go to find words suitable to a given situation. There is a heaven of gestures, too. Dos Passos makes a pretence of presenting gestures as pure events, as mere exteriors, as free, animal movements. But this is only appearance. Actually, in relating them, he adopts the point of view of the chorus, of public opinion. There is no single one of Dick's or of Eleanor's gestures which is not a public demonstration, performed to a humming accompaniment of flattery.

At Chantilly they went through the chateau and fed the big carp in the moat. They ate their lunch in the woods, sitting on rubber cushions. J. W. kept everybody laughing explaining how he hated picnics, asking everybody what it was that got into even the most intelligent women that they were always trying to make people go on picnics. After lunch they drove out to Senlis to see the houses that the Uhlans had destroyed there in the battle of the Marne.

Doesn't it sound like a local newspaper's account of an ex-servicemen's banquet? All of a sudden, as the gesture dwindles until it is no more than a thin film, we see that it *counts,* that it is sacred in character and that, at the same time, it involves commitment. But for whom? For the abject consciousness of "everyman", for what Heidegger calls "das Mann." But still, where does it spring from? Who is its representative as I read? *I* am. In order to understand the words, in order to make sense out of the paragraphs, I first have to adopt his point of view. I have to play the role of the obliging chorus. This consciousness exists only through me; without me there would be nothing but black spots on white paper. But even while I *am* this collective consciousness, I want to wrench away from it, to see it from the judge's point of view, that is, to get free of myself. This is the source of the shame and uneasiness with which Dos Passos knows how to fill the reader. I am a reluctant accomplice (though I am not even sure that I am reluctant), creating and rejecting social taboos. I am, deep in my heart, a revolutionary again, an unwilling one.

In return, how I hate Dos Passos' men! I am given a fleeting glimpse of their minds, just enough to see that they are living animals. Then, they begin to unwind their endless tissue of ritual statements and sacred gestures. For them, there is no break between inside and outside, between body and consciousness, but only between stammerings of an individual's timid, intermittent, fumbling thinking and the messy world of collective representations. What a simple process this is, and how effective! All one need do is use American journalistic technique in telling the story of a life, and like the Salzburg reed, a life crystallizes into the Social, and the problem of the transition to the typical—stumbling-block of the social novel—is thereby resolved. There is no further need to present a working man type, to compose (as Nizan does in *Antoine Bloyé*) an existence which represents the exact average of thousands of existences. Dos Passos, on the contrary, can give all his attention to rendering a single life's special character. Each of his characters is unique; what happens to him could happen to no one else. What does it matter, since Society has marked him more deeply than could any special circumstance, since *he is* Society? Thus, we get a glimpse of an order beyond the accidents of fate or the contigency of detail, an order more supple than Zola's physiological necessity or Proust's psychological mechanism, a soft and insinuating constraint which seems to release its victims, letting them go only to take possession of them again without their suspecting, in other words, a statistical determinism. These men, submerged in their own existences, live as they can. They struggle; what comes their way is not determined in advance. And yet, neither their efforts, their faults, nor their most extreme violence can interfere with the regularity of births, marriages and suicides. The pressure exerted by a gas on the walls of its container does not depend upon the individual histories of the molecules composing it.

We are still on the other side of the looking-glass. Yesterday you saw your best friend and expressed to him your passionate hatred of war. Now try to relate this conversation to yourself in the style of Dos Passos. "And they ordered two beers and said that war was hateful. Paul declared he would rather do anything than fight and John said he agreed with him and both got excited and said they were glad they agreed. On his way home, Paul decided to see John more often." You will start hating yourself immediately. It will not take you long, however, to decide that you *cannot* use this tone in talking about yourself. However insincere you may have been, you were at least living out your insincerity, playing it out on your own, continuously creating and extending its existence from one moment to the next. And even if you got caught up in collective representations, you had first to experience them as personal resignation.

We are neither mechanical objects nor possessed souls, but something worse; we are free. We exist either entirely *within* or entirely *without*. Dos Passos' man is a hybrid creature, an interior-exterior being. We go on living with him and within him, with his vacillating, individual consciousness, when suddenly it wavers, weakens, and is diluted in the collective consciousness. We follow it up to that point and suddenly, before we notice, we are on the outside. The man behind the looking-glass is a strange, contemptible, fascinating creature. Dos Passos knows how to use this constant shifting to find effect. I know of nothing more gripping than Joe's death.

> Joe laid out a couple of frogs and was backing off towards the door, when he saw in the mirror that a big guy in a blouse was bringing down a bottle on his head held with both hands. He tried to swing around but he didn't have time. The bottle crashed his skull and he was out.

We are inside with him, until the shock of the bottle on his skull. Then, immediately, we find ourselves outside with the chorus, part of the collective memory, ". . . and he was out." Nothing gives you a clearer feeling of annihilation. And from then on, each page we turn, each page that tells of other minds and of a world going on with Joe, is like a spadeful of earth over our bodies. But it is a behind-the-looking-glass death: all we really get is the fine *appearance* of nothingness. True nothingness can neither be felt or thought. Neither you nor I, nor anyone after us, will ever have anything to say about our real deaths.

Dos Passos' world—like those of Faulkner, Kafka, and Stendhal—is impossible because it is contradictory. But therein lies its beauty. Beauty is a veiled contradiction. I regard Dos Passos as the greatest writer of our time.

(August 1938)

Alfred Kazin

From *On Native Grounds*

Technically *U.S.A.* is one of the great achievements of the modern novel, yet what that achievement is can easily be confused with its elaborate formal structure. For the success of Dos Passos's method does not rest primarily on his schematization of the novel into four panels, four levels of American experience—the narrative proper, the "Camera Eye," the "Biographies," and the "Newsreel." That arrangement, while original enough, is the most obvious thing in the book and soon becomes the most mechanical. The book lives by its narrative style, the wonderfully concrete yet elliptical prose which bears along and winds around the life stories in the book like a conveyor belt carrying Americans through some vast Ford plant of the human spirit. *U.S.A.* is a national epic, the first great national epic of its kind in the modern American novel; and its triumph is not the pyrotechnical display that the shuttling between the various devices seems to suggest, but Dos Passos's power to weave so many different lives together in narrative. It is possible that the narrative sections would lose much of that power if they were not so craftily built into the elaborate framework of the book. But the framework holds the book together and encloses it; the narrative makes it. The "Newsreel" sounds the time; the "Biographies" stand above time, chanting the stories of American leaders; the "Camera Eye" moralizes shyly in a lyric stammer upon them. But the great thing about *U.S.A.* is that though it sweeps up so many human lives together and intones their waste and illusion and defeat so steadily, we seem to be swept along with them and to see each life perfectly at the moment it passes by us.

The brilliance of the structure lies therefore not so much in its external surface design as in its internal one, in the manifold rhythms of the narrative. Each of the various narrative sections has its dominant musical mode, as it were; each of the characters is encased in his characteristic prose. Thus at the very beginning of *The 42nd Parallel,* when the "Newsreel" blares in a welcome to the new century, while General Miles falls off his horse and Senator Beveridge's toast

From *On Native Grounds* (New York: Reynal and Hitchcock, 1942), 353-59, by Alfred Kazin. Copyright 1942, 1970, by Alfred Kazin. Reprinted by permission of Harcourt Brace Jovanovich, Inc. and the author.

to the new imperialist America is heard, the story of Fenian McCreary, "Mac," begins with the smell of whale-oil soap in the printer's house in Middletown. That smell, the clatter of the presses, the political arguments, the muddy streets and saloons, give the tone of Mac's life from the first, as his life—Wobbly, tramp, working stiff—sounds the emergence of labor as a dominant force in the new century. So the story of Eleanor Stoddard begins with "When she was small she hated everything," a sentence that calls up the thin-lipped rebellion and superciliousness, the artiness and desperation, of her loveless life before we have gone into it. *The 42nd Parallel* is a study in youth, of the youth of the new century, the "new America," and of all the human beings who figure in it; and it is in the world of Mac's bookselling and life on freights, of Eleanor Stoddard's rebellion against her father and Janey Williams's picnic near the falls at Georgetown, of J. Ward Moorehouse's Wilmington and the railroad boarding house Charley Anderson's mother kept in North Dakota, that we move. The narrator behind his "Camera Eye" is a little boy holding to his mother's hand, listening to his father's boasts (at the end of the book he will be on his way to France); the "Newsreel" sings out the headlines and popular songs of 1900-16; the "Biographies" are the magnates (Minor C. Keith, Carnegie), the wonder men of the new century (Steinmetz, Edison, Burbank), the rebels (Bryan, Debs, Bob La Follette, Big Bill Haywood).

We have just left the world of childhood behind us in *The 42nd Parallel,* but we can already hear the clatter of the conveyor belt pushing all these lives along. Everyone is sparring hard for position; the fences of life are going up. There is no expectancy in this youth, not even the sentimental poetry of adolescence. The "Newsreel" singing the lush ballads of 1906 already seems very far away; the "Biographies" are effigies in stone. The life in the narrative has become dominant; the endless pulsing drowns everything else out. Everything is hard, dry, and already a little outrageous. Johnny Moorehouse falls in love only to learn that the socially prominent girl whom he needs for his ambition is a whore. When Eleanor Stoddard's father announces his plan to marry again, he tells her it will be to a "Mrs. O'Toole, a widow with five children who kept a boardinghouse out Elsden way." Mac, after his bitterly hard youth, leaves the Wobblies with whom he has found comradeship and the joy of battle to marry a girl who drives him almost insane; then leaves her and is thrown into the Mexican revolutions of the period. Janey Williams's life has already taken on the gray color of the offices in which she will spend her life. There are no refuges in this world, no evasions, and above

all no second starts. The clamps have been laid down early, and
for all time.

Yet we can feel the toneless terror of all these lives, the oppression
and joylessness that seem to beat down upon us from the first, only
because every narrative section is so concrete and every sentence,
as Delmore Schwartz pointed out, "can expand in the reader's mind
to include a whole context of experience." *U.S.A.* is perhaps the first
great naturalistic novel that is primarily a triumph of style. Everything that lives in the book is wound up on the spool of that style;
from the fragments of popular songs in the "Newsreel" and the clean
verse structure of the "Biographies" down to the pounding beat of
the narrative, the book seems to be propelled by one dynamic rhythm.
The Dos Passos prose, once so uncertain and self-conscious, has here
been whittled down to a sharpness that can kill; but it has by no
means lost its old wistful rhetoric in *U.S.A.*, which is particularly
conspicuous in the impressionist "Camera Eye" sections, and generally gives a kind of secret and mischievous color to the severely
reportorial prose. Scrubby, slangy, with a kind of grim straightfor-
wardness, it is the style of a very cunning artisan who seems to be
working in these human materials as another might work in stone
or wood—forever carving away, forever whittling, but never without
subtle turns and a loving sense of design. It is never a "distinguished"
style, beautiful in its own right; never as prismatic as Fitzgerald's
or as delicately molded as Hemingway's, and there is always something fundamentally mechanical about it. But it is the style Dos
Passos needs to turn the motor of the conveyor belt; it is the reportorial and satiric style needed to push along and circumscribe all
these lives. With *The 42nd Parallel* we have entered into a machine
world in which the rhythm of the machine has become the primal
beat of all the people in it; and Dos Passos's hard, lean, mocking
prose, forever sounding that beat, calling them to their deaths, has
become the supreme expression of his conception of them.

Perhaps nowhere in the trilogy, save in the descending spiral of
Charley Anderson's life in the first half of *The Big Money,* is Dos
Passos's use of symbolic rhythm so brilliant as in the story of Joe
Williams in *1919.* For Joe, Janey Williams's sailor brother, is the
leading protagonist of the war and the early postwar period, as J.
Ward Moorehouse's ambitiousness marked the pattern of *The 42nd
Parallel.* Joe's endless shuttling between the continents on rotting
freighters has become the migration and rootlessness of the young
American generation whom we saw growing up in *The 42nd Parallel;*
and the growing stupor and meaninglessness of his life became the

leit-motif of the waste and death that hold everyone in the book
as in a ghostly vise. The theme of death, of the false optimism
immediately after the Armistice, are sounded immediately by the
narrator behind his "Camera Eye" reporting the death of his mother
and notation on the coming of peace—"tomorrow I hoped would be
the first day of the first month of the first year." The "Biographies"
are all studies in death and defeat, from Randolph Bourne to Wesley
Everest, mutilated and lynched after the Centralia shootings in
Washington in 1919; from the prose poem commemorating the dozens
of lives the Unknown Soldier might have led to the death's-head
portrait of J. P. Morgan ("Wars and panics on the stock exchange,/
machinegunfire and arson/ . . . starvation, lice, cholera and typhus").
The "Camera Eye" can detect only "the almond smell of high explo-
sives sending singing éclats through the sweetish puking grandilo-
quence of the rotting dead." And sounding its steady beat under
the public surface of war is the story of Joe Williams hurled between
the continents—Joe, the supreme Dos Passos cipher and victim and
symbol, suffering his life with dumb unconsciousness of how outrageous his life is, and continually loaded and dropped from one ship
to another like a piece of cargo.

> Twentyfive days at sea on the steamer *Argyle,* Glasgow, Captain
> Thompson, loaded with hides, chipping rust, daubing red lead on steel
> plates that were sizzling hot griddles in the sun, painting the stack
> from dawn to dark, pitching and rolling in the heavy dirty swell; bedbugs
> in the bunks in the stinking focastle, slumgullion for grub, with potatoes
> full of eyes and mouldy beans.

All through *1919* one can hear death being sounded. Every life
in it, even J. Ward Moorehouse's, has become a corrosion, a slow
descent. Richard Ellsworth Savage goes back on his early idealism
and becomes a cynical but willing abetter in Moorehouse's schemes.
Eveline Hutchins and Eleanor Stoddard lose all their genteel pretense
to art and grapple for Moorehouse's favor. "Daughter," the Texas
girl Savage has betrayed, falls to her death in an airplane. Even
Ben Compton, the New York radical, soon finds himself rotting away
in prison. The war for almost all of them has become an endless
round of drink and travel; they have brought nothing to it and learned
nothing from it save a growing consciousness of their futility. And
when they all slip into the twenties and the boom with *The Big
Money,* the story of Charley Anderson's precipitate rise and fall
becomes the last mad parable of their existence, a carnival of greed
and corruption. Beginning with Dick Savage's life on ambulances

and trains over France and Italy in *1919,* the pace of the trilogy
has become faster and faster; now, as the war world empties into
the pleasure world of *The Big Money*—New York and Detroit, Hollywood and Miami at the height of the boom—it has become a death
ride. There is money in the air, money and power for Charley Anderson and Margo Dowling and Dick Savage; but as they come closer
to this material triumph, their American dream, the machine has
begun to spin them too rapidly. Charley Anderson can kiss the bright
new century notes in his wallet, Margo can rise higher and higher
in Hollywood, Dick Savage, having sold out completely, can enjoy
his power at the hands of J. Ward Moorehouse; the machine has
begun to strangle them; there is no joy here for anyone. All through
The Big Money we wait for the balloon to collapse, for the death
cry we hear in the last drunken drive of Charley Anderson's and
his smashup.

What Waldo Frank said of Mencken is particularly relevant to
Dos Passos: he brings energy to despair. Not merely does the writing
in the trilogy become richer and firmer as the characters descend
into the pit, but Dos Passos himself seems so imbued with an almost
mystical conviction of failure that he rises to new heights in those
last sections of *The Big Money* which depict the last futile efforts
of the liberals and radicals to save Sacco and Vanzetti, and their
later internecine quarrels. The most moving scene in all of *U.S.A.*
is the scene in which Mary French, the only counterpoise to the
selfishness of the other characters in *The Big Money,* becomes so
exhausted by her labors for Sacco and Vanzetti that when she goes
to bed she dreams that the whole world is forever coming apart,
that she is climbing up a shaky hillside "among black guttedlooking
houses pitching at crazy angles where steelworkers lived" and being
thrown back. The conflicting hopes of Mary French, who wanted
Socialism, and of Charley Anderson, who wanted the big money, have
brought two different kinds of failure; but it is failure that broods
over them and over everyone else in *U.S.A.* in the end—over the
pompous fakes like J. Ward Moorehouse, the radicals like Ben
Compton, the grasping little animals like Eleanor Stoddard and
Eveline Hutchins, the opportunists like Richard Ellsworth Savage.
The two survivors are Margo Dowling, supreme for the moment in
Hollywood, and the homeless boy "Vag," who stands alone on the
Lincoln Highway, gazing up at the transcontinental plane above
winging its way west, the plane full of solid and well-fed citizens
glittering in the American sun, the American dream. *All right we
are two nations.* And like the scaffolding of hell in *The Divine Comedy,*

they are frozen into eternity; for Dos Passos there is nothing else, save the integrity of the camera eye that must see this truth and report it, the integrity and sanctity of the individual locked up in the machine world of modern society.

With *The Big Money,* published at the height of the nineteen-thirties, the story of the twenties comes to a close; but even more does it bring the story of the lost generation to a close, that generation which has stood at the peak of modern time in America as no other has. Here in *U.S.A.,* in the most ambitious of all its works, is its measure of the national life, its conception of history—and it is a history of struggle that is vain, of failure that is irrevocable, and of final despair. There is strength in *U.S.A.,* Dos Passos's own strength, the strength of the craft that can weld so many lives together and make them live so intensely before us as they pass. But for the rest it is a brilliant hecatomb, and one of the coldest and most mechanical of tragic novels. By the time we have come to the end of *U.S.A.* we begin to feel what Edmund Wilson could detect in Dos Passos before it appeared, that "his disapproval of capitalistic society becomes a distaste for all the human beings who compose it." The protest, the lost-generation "I," has taken all of them into his vision; he has given us his truth. Yet if it intones anything affirmative in the end, it is the pronouncement of young Orestes Brownson—"There is no such thing as reforming the mass without reforming the individuals who compose it." It is this conviction, rising to a bitter crescendo in *Adventures of a Young Man,* this unyielding protest against modern society on the part of a writer who has now turned back to the roots of "our storybook democracy" in works like *The Ground We Stand On* and his projected life of Thomas Jefferson, that separates Dos Passos from so many of the social novelists who follow after him in the thirties. Where he speaks of sanctity, they speak of survival; where he lives by the truth of the camera eye, they live *in* the vortex of that society which Dos Passos has always been able to measure, with hatred but not in panic, from the outside. Dos Passos is the first of the new naturalists, and *U.S.A.* is the dominant social novel of the thirties; but it is not merely a vanished social period that it commemorates: it is an individualism, a protestantism, a power of personal disassociation, that seem almost to speak from another world.

John W. Aldridge

From *After the Lost Generation*

It is generally believed that the bitterness engendered in Dos Passos by the injustice done to Sacco and Vanzetti provided him with the focus and purpose he needed to write his immense trilogy *U.S.A.* However true this may be, one can just as easily explain his achievement in that work in terms of natural creative evolution. As we have already seen, there were two distinct forces developing in Dos Passos' work up to the time of *U.S.A. One Man's Initiation* was primarily a record of his early disenchantment with the ideals of war and his emerging sympathy with the victims of war. *Three Soldiers* was an open protest against the evils of war at the same time that it indicated the futility of the individual's revolt against the system responsible for the making of wars. In *Manhattan Transfer* Dos Passos' social sympathies had broadened to such an extent that he was able to depict the futility he felt in terms of a dozen lives; but his disenchantment rendered those lives meaningless. They did not add up to a powerful denunciation of the system—because Dos Passos had still not found a way of centering his sympathies on an object more precise than that of the undifferentiated human mass. But as the result of the experiments he made in *Manhattan Transfer,* Dos Passos was able to return to the material he had begun to explore in that book and see in it implications which had previously escaped him. He sensed now that the real victims of the system were the working classes and that the real evils of the system stemmed from wealth and power. He was thus able to focus his sympathies upon a specific social group and set them against his hatred of another social group, just as in his earlier work he had focused his sympathies upon the individual aesthete and set them against his hatred of war. He was able to write now within the frame of two distinct and separate worlds, two nations, and to bring to his writing the full power of his protest (for he believed in the cause of the working classes as he had formerly believed in the cause of the aesthete) as well as the full power of his futility (for he knew, in spite of his belief in their cause, that the working classes under capitalism must always be defeated.)

Reprinted from *After the Lost Generation* (New York: McGraw-Hill, 1951), pp. 71-76, by permission of the author. Copyright 1951 by John W. Aldridge.

The dramatic intensity of *U.S.A.* derives from the perfect balance of these conflicting forces within Dos Passos. There is, on one side, the gradual corruption and defeat of the characters whose lives are depicted in the straight-narrative sections. There is, on the other, the implicit indignation of the harsh, cutting style, which runs persistently counter to the drift of the narrative and comments upon it. Then, in the "Camera Eye" and "Biographies" sections the style picks up additional counterforce. The lyric meditations of the "Camera Eye" recast in poetic terms the negation expressed in the narrative and serve as a sort of moral center for the book. Through them the author periodically reenters the book and reminisces on moments out of the past when men fought, and were punished for fighting, for the cause of labor. During these moments, he seems to be saying, occurred the real tragedy of which the characters are now victims. The "Biographies" comment on the narrative in still other terms. This time the portraits are of real men who have been instrumental in shaping the system, either by rebelling against it or by trying to dominate it. Those who have rebelled are, for the most part, martyrs to the cause—Debs, Veblen, Big Bill Haywood, Randolph Bourne, Sacco and Vanzetti. Those who have sought power are, for the most part, tycoons like Hearst, Carnegie, and J. P. Morgan. But, however much their aims may have differed, the destiny of both groups is the same: the rebels are defeated by the system and the tycoons are corrupted by it.

This hypothesis of universal ruin, introduced lyrically through the "Camera Eye" and historically through the "Biographies," is given dramatic proof in the narrative proper. Here all the social classes of *U.S.A.* are represented. There are J. Ward Moorehouse, Charley Anderson, Richard Ellsworth Savage, Eveline Hutchins, Eleanor Stoddard, the prototypes of privilege; and Joe Williams, Ben Compton, Mary French, the prototypes of unprivilege. Each has a different story, but all come to the same end.

The career of J. Ward Moorehouse, the central symbol of Dos Passos' American-dream-become-nightmare, links the three volumes of the trilogy together into one continuous narrative. Born near the turn of the century, Moorehouse is the typical product of the new industrial Success Myth. Like Fitzgerald's Gatsby, he begins early in youth to build his life around the simple pioneer virtues of Horatio Alger: early rising, hard work, thrift, honesty, self-confidence—"By gum, I can do it." His story, beginning in *The 42nd Parallel,* is a perfect leitmotiv for the naive new century; and it is presented, fittingly enough, against a background of jubilantly patriotic headlines, "Biographies" of the new wonder men of science (Edison, Burbank, Steinmetz) and the new political rebels (Bryan, LaFollette, Debs, Big Bill Haywood), and lyric reveries of the "Camera Eye" narrator, who is still a child. But out of this background the stories of other youths also emerge. Mac, the boy who never had a chance, begins as a seller of pornographic books, drifts aimlessly over the country looking for work, gets a girl in trouble, leaves her to become a revolutionary comrade in Mexico; Janey Williams goes to work, gets lost in the gray office routine that is to be her life; Eleanor Stoddard, thin, sterile, hater of everything and everyone, struggles to get ahead as an interior decorator. And finally we see that the sickness which has begun to destroy these people almost from the moment of their birth has infected Moorehouse also. No longer the innocent trusting child of the new century, he has become a perversion of its ideals and a burlesque of his own earlier hopes. After divorcing his socially prominent wife because she is a whore, he begins to perfect his talent for exploiting the talents of others. Janey Williams as his secretary, Eleanor Stoddard as his platonic mistress, and Eveline Hutchins as Eleanor's best friend all come under his influence and are carried forward by him toward a success that is to be their common grave.

As Moorehouse's ambition characterizes *The 42nd Parallel,* so the aimless drifting of Joe Williams, Janey's brother, sets the pattern for *1919,* the year that marked the beginning of the end of the Great American Dream for Dos Passos. As Joe wanders from continent to continent, getting drunk, whoring, fighting, hating, the generation he symbolizes plunges headlong into the violence of the Boom years. The "Biographies" now are studies in horror and destruction (Jack Reed, dead of typhus in Moscow; the ghost of Randolph Bourne "crying out in a shrill soundless giggle/*War is the health of the state";* Woodrow Wilson, idealist and dreamer, broken on the cause of Peace; J. P. Morgan—"Wars and panics on the stock exchange,/ machinegunfire and arson,/bankruptcies, warloans,/starvation, lice, cholera, and typhus:/good growing weather for the House of Morgan"; Joe Hill executed). The "Camera Eye" narrator is no longer a child but a disillusioned ex-soldier "walking the streets rolling on your bed eyes sting from peeling the speculative onion of doubt if somebody in your head topdog? underdog? didn't (and on Union Square "say liar to you"). Richard Ellsworth Savage, one-time idealist and poet, becomes a Moorehouse underling; Eveline Hutchins and Eleanor Stoddard fight for their share of the Moorehouse patronage; "Daughter," the reforming young Texas girl whom Savage has ruined, is killed in a plane crash; Ben Compton, the hard-working radical, is jailed. The forming patterns of *The 42nd Parallel* have now hardened into a mold; the pace has become faster and more frantic; and the hunger for success has become a mad lust for pleasure and power.

The corruption, greed and spiritual torment of the years after the war shroud *The Big Money* in an atmosphere of chilly death. For nearly all the characters the American Dream has found a monstrous apotheosis in material triumph. Charley Anderson makes money, more money than he ever imagined existed in the world, but finds no happiness. Margo Dowling, after a life of incredible sordidness culminating in high-class prostitution, rises to spectacular success in Hollywood; J. Ward Moorehouse, grown old and empty, finally perceives his failure, collapses, and dies; Savage, realizing too late that he has sold out his ideals, sinks into homosexual corruption. The "Biographies" too have become portraits of waste and misused success (Frederick Winslow Taylor, the efficiency expert, who "never saw the working of the American plan" and who died with his watch in his hand; Hearst, "a spent Caesar grown old with spending/never man enough to cross the Rubicon"; Henry Ford, the mechanical wizard, living a frightened old age surrounded by "thousands of millionaire acres, protected by an army of servicemen, secretaries, secret agents, dicks under orders of an English exprizefighter . . . ," attempting to "put back the old bad road, so that everything might be the way it used to be, in the days of horses and buggies"; Veblen, dying unrecognized, deliberately obliterating the last traces of his own memory—"It is also my wish . . . that no tombstone, slab, epitaph, effigy, tablet, inscription or monument be set up to my memory or name in any place or at any time; that no obituary, memorial, portrait, or biography of me . . . be printed or published"). Finally, at the end, in Charley Anderson's crack-up, the destruction is made pathetically complete and the last ideals of a great age are brought to ruin. There is only "Vag" now, the hopeless, embittered wanderer, hitchhiking, like Jimmy Herf, to nowhere on the big concrete highway; while overhead an air liner passes filled with transcontinental passengers thinking "contracts, profits, vacation-trips, mighty continent between Atlantic and Pacific, power, wires humming dollars, cities jammed, hills empty, the Indian-trail leading into the wagonroad, the macadamed pike, the concrete skyway, trains, planes: history the billiondollar speedup. . . . *All right we are two nations.*"

The U.S.A. which Dos Passos describes is thus more than simply a country or a way of life. It is a condition of death, a wasteland

of futility and emptiness. In it, the best and the worst must be
defeated; for defeat can be the only answer for the inhabitants of
a world in which all goals are unattainable and the most powerful
gods are corrupt. Yet, although the thing he describes is death, Dos
Passos brings to his description a savage kind of power which saves
it from becoming dead too. Through it all, he has consistently hated
and condemned; and he has expressed his hatred with great strength
and purpose. This has given meaning to the meaninglessness of his
characters, value to their valuelessness. His style has been the perfect
instrument of that meaning, protesting at every step in its development against the horror of the thing it was disclosing. His "Camera
Eye" and biographical devices have extended that meaning to the
outermost limits of suggestion and elevated it to the stature of pure
insight into the dilemma of our time. What was shadowy and unfocused in *Manhattan Transfer* is now brilliantly clear; the protest
has broken free of the mere mass and become concentrated in a
specific social phenomenon; and as this has occurred, Dos Passos
has also been freed, to create the world of powerful despair which
is his best and truest world.

Blanche H. Gelfant

The Fulfillment of Form in U. S. A.

Behind *U.S.A.* is the same emotional impetus, the same burning
vision of modern decadence, and the same sense of urgency that
underlie *Manhattan Transfer*. But Dos Passos wrote *U.S.A.* with
the experience of *Manhattan Transfer* behind him. And he had
learned from this experience. Whether or not he realized it, *Manhattan Transfer* was the preliminary apprentice-piece for his masterwork,
U.S.A. The earlier novel helped bring his creative faculties to the
point of their fullest development, and the fruition of his talents,
the fulfillment of the form he was seeking to embody and assess
the times, is displayed in the trilogy. Strictly speaking, *U.S.A.* is not

From *The American City Novel,* by Blanche Housman Gelfant (Norman: University
of Oklahoma Press), pp. 166-74. Copyright 1954 by the University of Oklahoma Press.
Reprinted by permission of the University of Oklahoma Press.

a city novel: it is a unique work that should not be confined to a limited category. But because it reveals Dos Passos' broad synoptic intention, and because it is, within a larger framework, one of the best revelations of urbanism as a way of life, it can legitimately be discussed here, even if only suggestively. The main purpose will be to show how Dos Passos carried over to *U.S.A.* the same ideas and intentions he had in *Manhattan Transfer,* while he transmuted, rather than changed, his literary methods.

Although *Manhattan Transfer* clearly reflected Dos Passos' aesthetic sensibility and social conscience, it was obvious that Dos Passos was trying to establish an impersonal relationship between himself and his work. He tried to make himself a sensitive camera lens that registered and reflected a complex scene; his purpose was to record a picture in its details and as it existed independent of himself as interpreter. The assumption was that if the picture was faithful to the essentials of reality, an intelligent observer could draw from it certain inevitable inferences. In *U.S.A.,* Dos Passos introduced the Camera Eye sections in order to permit himself a direct expression of personal views and emotions, while at the same time he maintained the separation between himself as recorder and the picture he was recording. Technically, the Camera Eye shows the perfection of his impressionistic method. These fleeting impressions that capture objective acts as well as the inner stream of consciousness have been reduced to essentials in order to achieve the heightened effect of concentration. We have only to compare the way the same scene is treated in *Manhattan Transfer* and in *U.S.A.* to realize how fully Dos Passos was now able to exploit the impressionistic method both for its economy and its effect of intensity. Thematically, the Camera Eye sections provide a keystone upon which the entire structure of the trilogy rests. Far from being the residual product of Dos Passos' poetic talents, as some critics claim, they are the immediate expression of his social and moral conscience. They contain the story of his growth to an awareness of the social tragedy overtaking the country. Here he reveals the quality of his own mind and experiences as well as the observations that led him to see that America was becoming self-divided, that its ideals of justice and freedom were being trampled underfoot.

It is in the Camera Eye section that he states explicitly his view that "America our nation has been beaten by strangers who have bought the laws and fenced off the meadows and cut down the woods for pulp and turned our pleasant cities into slums and sweated the wealth out of our people and when they want to they hire the executioner to throw the switch." The contrast between an idealistic past and the present, which is always implicit in his works, is clearly defined in these passages. The Camera Eye shows him standing at the historic spot where the immigrants, "the kingkillers haters of oppression," landed. He recalls the "threehundred years the immigrants toiled into the west," and then turns to the present to see "another immigrant . . . hater of oppression," Bartolomeo Vanzetti, hounded and killed.

The Camera Eye shows too the growth of his determination to speak out in the language of the artist in protest against this degradation of American ideals. As he leaves Boston, the scene of past acts of historic greatness and of the present injustice, he asks: "How can I make them feel how our fathers our uncles haters of oppression came to this coast how say Don't let them scare you how make them feel who are your oppressors America." It is the task of the artist to reconstitute the glorious phrases of the past that expressed our hopes and ideals—"to rebuild the ruined words worn slimy in the mouths of lawyers districtattorneys collegepresidents judges." This is what he has tried to do in *U.S.A.* by a kind of reverse process: he re-creates a shattered America in order to recall a past made great by an integrity of ideals. The artist himself does not belong within this picture of a society in decay, for he is the instrument through which the picture is projected. Moreover, although he has emerged from this society, he cannot be identified with it or considered part of it, for he has rejected it by his disapproval and his refusal to conform to its pattern. The difference between the artist who has become a Camera Eye that reflects and judges the social scene and the people who are part of the scene is, then, an essential one; and it is maintained by an actual division within the trilogy.

Just as Dos Passos used urban symbols in *Manhattan Transfer* to represent the destructive forces in modern society, he uses here prominent twentiety-century men to symbolize the two opposing factions of a self-divided America. The particular aspect of American life these people represent is clearly secondary in importance to the social ideal and historical tendency they stand for. According to Dos Passos, America has become self-divided because of an inner conflict between social ideals. The resolution of this conflict will determine the destiny of the country, whether it will harden into a monopolistic society which crushes the common man and uses him as fodder for imperialistic war or into a true democracy which carries out our traditional ideals of justice and equality. Thorstein Veblen is Dos Passos' key figure not only because he represents specific social ideals that Dos Passos finds admirable but more important, because he describes with rare perspicuity the alternative forms American society can take. On the one hand, it can become "a warlike society strangled by the bureaucracies of the monopolies forced by the law of diminishing returns to grind down more and more the common man for profits"; or, on the other hand, it might become "a new matteroffact commonsense society dominated by the needs of the men and women who did the work and the incredibly vast possibilities for peace and plenty offered by the progress of technology."

Each person Dos Passos has selected for a biographical sketch in some way represents one of these alternatives and the ideals upon which it rests. Men like Minor Keith, Carnegie, Wilson, Morgan, Ford, Hearst, and Samuel Insull have impelled society in the direction of monopolism; wittingly or unwittingly, selfishly or misguidedly, they have fostered wars in foreign countries and hatred and oppression at home. They have guarded the interests of big business at the expense of the common man's liberty. They are the motive powers behind the lynchings, witch-hunts, and night-raids that were America's tragedy and disgrace. Opposed to them in principle and act are Dos Passos' defeated heroes: Eugene V. Debs, Big Bill Haywood, Bob LaFollette, Jack Reed, Randolph Bourne, Paxton Hibben, Joe Hill, Wesley Everest, Frank Lloyd Wright, and Thorstein Veblen. Dos Passos interprets even such a nonpolitical figure as Isadora Duncan as a symbol of the force that resists oppression and reaction. Like each of the men named above, she maintained integrity as an individual. Her integrity lay in being a free artist, in resisting not only the "philistines" who would not let her dance in America, but also the warmakers who would have her give up Wagner and support their "butchery." The test that Dos Passos has applied to each of his symbolic figures is whether or not they supported the war: if they did, they represent the historic force of oppression, and if they did not, they stand for the common cause of the people who are the force behind the progress towards democracy. Thus, Isadora Duncan represents not simply Art but the artist's love for the people, which makes him abhor oppression and its attendant evil, war: "She was an American like Walt Whitman; the murdering rulers of the world were not her people; the marchers were her people; artists were not on the side of the machineguns; she was an American in a Greek tunic; she was for the people."

The biographical sketches contain Dos Passos' most trenchant writing; and as we understand the profound symbolic meaning these people had for him, we can see why he was moved to the intenseness that makes his irony so brutally effective. In *Manhattan Transfer,* he had exerted the full force of his inventive and imaginative powers upon the urban symbols which stood for a manner of life and a process of social decay—both of which he deplored. But he was making symbols out of impersonal, and hence unmoral, elements; and he could not possibly feel towards the people in his sketches. He could respond to his contemporaries not merely as aesthetic elements but also as people who had moral responsibility and were therefore to be despised for their moral guilt or admired for their integrity. The emotions these people could evoke and focalize, and that a Skyscraper or a Rollercoaster could not, vitalize them as symbols. In *Manhattan Transfer,* Dos Passos was obviously fascinated by the possibilities for creating aesthetic patterns with the symbols, while here in *U.S.A.* the representative men are much more to him than aesthetic material. They are the very expression of his essential social beliefs, and as he portrays them, he is able finally to make his ideas, emotions, and expression one aesthetic integer.

The Newsreel sections re-create the newspaper of the times as a scanning reader might see them. They have both factual and atmospheric value: they tell us what is happening, and they also give us a sense of the social milieu. Their most serious shortcoming is not that they force an artificial separation between the narrative and its social background but that as an aesthetic unit in themselves, they are relatively uninteresting. While the subway-rider may flick through his newspaper with genuine interest, the novel-reader does not look for bare and undigested information, no matter how pertinent it may be to the fictitious action. Rather he anticipates the aesthetic pleasure which comes from finding artistic order in the material he reads. There can be no doubt that Dos Passos has carefully selected and arranged the newspaper excerpts, but both his objective in the Newsreel sections and the technique used to achieve it make it impossible for him to rise above the aesthetic limitations inherent in newspaper scanning. In *Manhattan Transfer,* he had made brief references to newspaper articles mainly for their factual value, while the atmosphere and tensions of the scene were re-created by the very movement and pace of the novel. The organization of *U.S.A.* into large narrative units dealing with one person prevents Dos Passos from attaining the atmospheric effects he achieved in *Manhattan Transfer* by handling the narrative in an irregular and discontinuous manner. Nevertheless, the narrative sections of *U.S.A.* succeed so well in capturing the quality of the mood of the milieu, as well as of the characters, that one really does not need to supplement them with Newsreel passages that give a sense of the times.

Perhaps the most brilliant achievement of the Newsreel sections is that as they provide a historical counterpart to the fictional sections, they make fiction more acceptable as truth than the accounts from real life. The Newsreels record such inanities, falsehoods, and ironic perversities that by contrast the inanities and ironies that are fictional begin to seem more true to life. The quality of the mass mentality revealed by the Newsreels would make us more willing to accept Dos Passos' characters not because they have the same quality of mind but because, if anything, they are on a higher level. No matter how sordid or selfish they are, they have managed at least not to sink to such acts of madness as the newspapers report nor to subscribe to such self-deceptions as the American leaders preach. Some of the remarks of Wilson, Taft, or Hoover that Dos Passos quotes here are beyond the talents of his characters most skilled in verbal legerdemain, Dick Savage and Ward Moorehouse. By placing fact and fiction in juxtaposition, Dos Passos has succeeded curiously in gaining for his fiction an assent which we are unwilling to give to facts.

Although in *U.S.A.* Dos Passos shows his people suffering from the same inner confusions and spiritual emptiness that had typified the characters of his earlier novel, *Manhattan Transfer,* he is much more successful in capturing their essential humanity as well as their individual manners. The larger narrative unit allows him to create a continuous identity for his characters, so that they are no longer merely vivid but fragmentary states of mind; and because he deals with them as continuous personalities, he succeeds better in showing their inner disintegration. The dramatic effectiveness of Dick Savage's moral collapse, for example, derives from the effectiveness with which Dos Passos has built him up as a character. His life appears to us as more than a series of unrelated moments; it is a patterned sequence in which we can trace the dissolutive process that transforms Dick from a rather idealistic youth into a hack and libertine. Dos Passos brings us into an immediate contact with his characters by adapting for each one of them a language directly expressive of the quality of his mind and sensibility. He writes the narrative in the idiom of the characters, thus creating them for us by the very style in which he describes them. His sheer mastery of the language of the people has never been demonstrated so impressively as in these narrative sections in which he has made successfully high aesthetic demands upon even the coarsest vulgate speech. Style can no longer be separated as a vehicle of expression: it has become character. His purpose is to achieve the highest degree of objectivity by withdrawing himself as narrator and allowing the characters to be the medium through which their stories receive expression. The effect of this is that each character exists as an almost completely self-sustained element, for the evidence of the outside personality of the creator, which might be contained in the style, has been obliterated.

Yet Dos Passos' highest achievement with his characters is not the vivid and immediate projection of their personalities. Rather, it is the perfect identification of the state of the human spirit with the spirit of the times. Charley Anderson is the age of "The Big Money," as is Ward Moorehouse, or Dick Savage at the end of the trilogy. Joe Williams and "Nineteen-Nineteen" are coterminous—we cannot tell at what point the identity of one is separate from that of the other. The people are the human correlatives of the historical moment. That helps to explain why we find them, for the most part, so offensive. The tragedy of their inner emptiness and ineffectuality is the social tragedy of what seemed to Dos Passos mad years of war and ignominious money-making. The hope we find in Mary French is the hope that the historic moment still offers us a chance to make a better society and a finer people. Dos Passos has created his characters, then, with a multiple consciousness; he is conscious of them as individual human beings, mainly worthy of our irony and disdain; he is conscious of them as being the social and historic times; he is conscious of them, also, as the part and the whole of the social tragedy of twentieth-century America.

Charles Child Walcutt

From *American Literary Naturalism: A Divided Stream*

The technique of *Manhattan Transfer* is inconspicuous beside that of the trilogy *U.S.A.* (1937), composed of three huge novels, *The 42nd Parallel* (1930), *Nineteen Nineteen* (1932), and *The Big Money* (1936). In these novels Dos Passos has extended his method of projecting the kaleidoscope to the point where he fashions his pattern out of

From Walcutt, Charles C., *American Literary Naturalism: A Divided Stream* pages 283-89. University of Minnesota Press, Minneapolis. © Copyright 1956, University of Minnesota. Reprinted by permission of the University of Minnesota Press and the author.

three elaborately contrived elements which interrupt and supplement the central narratives—the Newsreel, the Camera Eye, and the Biography. With this invention he seeks to find styles that are appropriate to the various types of material treated and that in blending give the effect of variousness, energy, and turmoil that we saw in a simpler way in *Manhattan Transfer*.

The body of the trilogy is devoted to the careers of a dozen representative people through the years from about the turn of this century to the big money days of the twenties. The first novel approaches World War I, the second deals largely with civilian activities during the war, in New York and Paris, the third explores the big money boom after the war. There is no central character in *U.S.A.* Each novel deals with about four of the dozen, and there is a slight carryover from one novel to the next. In *The 42nd Parallel* the main characters are Mac McCreary, son of a laborer, who struggles through the labor movement, joins and leaves the I.W.W. in the Northwest, and ends by living with a Mexican girl and comfortably selling radical books from their shop; J. Ward Moorehouse, from Delaware, who marries wealthy women, rises through business and public relations into politics, where he pompously mediates between capital and labor with the purpose of keeping the latter in line, and has a long platonic relation with Eleanor Stoddard, who is a frigid, frustrated, artistic, ambitious bitch from Chicago, comes to New York, where she prospers as an interior decorator, has an important position in the Red Cross in Paris (this is in the second volume), and finally marries a Russian prince; and Janey Williams, mousey and fearful, who becomes the devoted secretary of J. Ward Moorehouse.

Nineteen Nineteen adds the career of Janey's brother, Joe Williams, an ignorant bloke trying to get along, who joins the Navy, deserts, and brawls his way purposelessly through the action; Richard Ellsworth Savage, cultured and personable, who somehow drifts down into opportunism and debasement of his literary talents in J. Ward Moorehouse's employment, a kind of unhappy playboy; Eveline Hutchins, daughter of a Chicago minister who terrifies her, seduced by a Mexican painter, who joins Eleanor Stoddard for a while as interior decorator, goes with her to Paris, is jilted by the man she loves, has a brief affair with Moorehouse and another with a soldier named Paul, and later dies from a lethal dose of sleeping pills; and Daughter, a wild Texas tomboy who has a gay and frantic life spending her father's money and running from men, traveling abroad after the war, who transfers the early frustrated passion that has been the cause of her restlessness to Dick Savage, and who dies, pregnant and rejected by him, in an airplane crash.

The Big Money almost has a central character, Charley Anderson, aviator and war ace, who goes into business manufacturing airplanes and is on the way to riches when he is caught up in the fever of market speculation that takes his money as fast as he can make it. An airplane crash puts him out of circulation and he loses his part in the business; his drinking and gambling increase, and he dies in Florida after an automobile accident when he tried to beat a train to a crossing, going eighty-five miles an hour. Charley's is the grittiest and most desperate story in the whole trilogy. There are also Mary French, a spectacled student, drab and miserable, who devotes herself to Reform; and Margo Dowling, who works her busy, heartless way through a number of men to a fat contract in Hollywood.

These interweaving careers (all the characters know some of the others at one time or another) are given in larger segments than those in *Manhattan Transfer;* but always with a clinical detachment that makes them seem like figures on a screen compelled by drives the inwardness of which we never know, until finally we come to the conclusion that all their drives are instinctive or compulsive. The total effect is much like the strident chaos of the first novel.

The three devices which interrupt the central narratives and "formalize" the chaos depicted represent the ultimate stylistic expressiveness of the naturalistic movement. The Newsreel introduces a section with bits of headlines, advertisements, feature articles, and phrases of news, interwoven with lines of poetry which presumably represent some of the emotions—usually popular and sentimental—being experienced at the time. Superficially, it represents a world of fraud and sophistication, violence and treachery; it is a backdrop of hysteria behind which the serious business of society, if such it can be called, is concealed; for high finance and international relations continue to control the world while the public is engaged with sentiment and sensation.

The Biographies—there are twenty-five of them scattered through the three volumes—are condensed records of typical public figures of the time, from the fields of business, politics, technology, labor, and the arts. Such figures as Carnegie, Hearst, Insull, Rudolph Valentino, Isadora Duncan, William Jennings Bryan, and Eugene Debs constitute a sampling of specific figures who dominate the stage and also move the properties and scenes of our time. They are set forth ironically and bitterly, for the businessmen are greedy and unscrupulous, the entertainers are victims of their public as well as panders to its lusts and vanities, the liberal politicians are confused by their ambitions and the inadequacies of their idealism, and the efficiency expert (F. W. Taylor) is an inhuman machine who dies with a stop watch in his hand. If these are the public heroes, the images of greatness which they portray for the common man—through the jittery glittering Newsreel show why "our storybook democracy" has not come true. The one figure presented by Dos Passos with a devotion approaching reverence is Thorstein Veblen, the lonely and satiric analyst of leisure-class conduct and the sabotage of efficiency by rapacious business, who could not fit into our academic world and who died leaving the request that his ashes be scattered into the sea and no monument or memorial of any sort be erected to his name.

The Camera Eye is Dos Passos' subjective and rather poetic commentary on this world. It occurs fifty-one times through the trilogy, revealing the character, interests, and life history of the artist—how he came out of Virginia, went to school abroad and at Harvard, drove an ambulance during the war, was disillusioned by the Versailles Treaty and the rampage of materialism which followed it, and lived as a newspaper reporter and radical through the big money days of the early twenties. He is an oversensitive and fastidious intellectual, recoiling from the grubby masses and yet seeing in them the backbone and heart of the America which the great sweep of his novel shows being corrupted, debauched, and enslaved by the forces of commercial rapacity. He sees America through the lens of a poetic tradition—Whitman, Sandburg, perhaps Hart Crane—which impels him to identify the physical elements of our nation with the dream of greatness and individual realization that it has always embodied for the transcendentalist.

Here the characteristics I have attributed to American idealism when it breaks away from its scientific discipline and control—of unfocused idealism and uncontrolled protest—become increasingly evident in the notions that virtue is in the people, waste is the natural expression of the exploiters, and wealth is in a long-term conspiracy to sabotage labor and destroy our resources. It is perhaps not extravagant to identify the perfectly expressive form of this work with the final division of the great stream of American idealism. The form expresses a chaos; it is a fractured world pictured in a novel fractured into four parts through four styles from four points of view. This division of the subject combines with the range and variety of the materials treated to give the impression that nothing can be done because the problem is too complex to take hold of. It can be watched in the frantic samples that Dos Passos gives us, but we get no sense of comprehensible process that might be analyzed and controlled by the application of scientific method, because it is, finally, a *moral* deterioration that Dos Passos depicts. Thus with the radical writer we come full circle to the conservative position.

The point can be illustrated by samples of the Camera Eye taken from *The Big Money:* returning from Europe,

> throat tightens when the redstacked steamer churning the faintly-heaving slatecolored swell swerves shaking in a long greenmarbled curve past the red lightship.
> spine stiffens with the remembered chill of the offshore Atlantic
> and the jag of framehouses in the west above the invisible land and spiderweb rollercoasters and the chewinggum towers of Coney and the freighters with their stacks way aft and the blur beyond Sandy Hook
> and the vision spreads over the nation, to
> the whine and shriek of the buzzsaw and the tipsy smell of raw lumber and straggling through slagheaps through fireweed through wasted woodlands the shantytowns the shantytowns

He refuses a profitable job because he cannot become part of the exploiting machine, talks with other seekers in Greenwich Village, listens skeptically to orators in Union Square, identifies himself in Whitmanesque fashion with hunters and adventurers in the West, and toward the end makes a pilgrimage to Plymouth to hear about Sacco and Vanzetti.

> pencil scrawls in my notebook the scraps of recollection the broken halfphrases the effort to intersect word with word to dovetail clause with clause to rebuild out of mangled memories unshakably (Oh Pontius Pilate) the truth . . .
> . . . how can I make them feel our fathers our uncles haters of oppression came to this coast   how say   Don't let them scare you how make them feel who are your oppressors America
> rebuild the ruined words worn slimy in the mouths of lawyers district-attorneys collegepresidents judges   without the old words the immigrants haters of oppression brought to Plymouth how can you know who are your betrayers America

And the final cry of denunciation:

> they have clubbed us off the streets   they are stronger   they are rich they hire and fire the politicians the newspapereditors the old judges . . . America will not forget her betrayers . . .
> America our nation has been beaten by strangers who have bought the laws and fenced off the meadows and cut down the woods for pulp

and turned our pleasant cities into slums and sweated the wealth out
of our people . . .
  we stand defeated America

The trouble here is that the indictment has been torn loose from
the facts. People are not virtuous because they are poor. If we choose
to be sentimental about trees, it was the poor pioneer who cut down
and burned the hardwood forests over half a continent, a fearful
waste, whereas the big corporations that cut the pulpwood conserve
their trees carefully and have over the decades increased their reserves
beyond the nation's needs. The prairies were gulched by the poor
farming and overgrazing of the pioneers, too, long before they were
fenced and restored and protected by the avaricious big money farmers.

Particularly significant of this division and confusion is the fact
that most of the central characters are sexually frigid, inhibited,
deprived, or frustrated. Margo Dowling is unfeeling; Janey is terrified
of sex; Eleanor Stoddard is apparently quite frigid; Daughter is
confused and repressed, and her sudden passion for Dick Savage
causes her destruction; Mary French is completely inhibited and
neurotic. Where the sexual life is presumed to be satisfactory, Dos
Passos ignores it, but with the others a substantial preoccupation
of the author is to explore the fears, the desolation, and the guilty
aimlessness which he relates to the sense of being unloved. This
preoccupation gives the book a pervasive dreariness which combines
with the fact that people seem always to be smoky, grimy, gritty,
and tired to make a desolation that is, ultimately, wholly subjective.
It is a literary effect contrived by careful selection of detail and
control of language.

It is true that the possessors of great wealth and power have abused
both, and yet he has loaded the dice so heavily in favor of the common
man that the reader is skeptical when Dos Passos is most earnest.
His idealism has lost its hold on fact. The result, as usual, shows
the facts (in the stream of materialism) as grim, dark, and uncon-
trollable, whereas the optimism of spirit is dissipated in fierce but
unreliable indignation. The form of this trilogy is a perfect embodi-
ment of this division between nature and spirit: the main blocks
of the narrative portray characters groping in a hopeless jungle of
sensation and instinct, whereas the Camera Eye cries its somewhat
irresponsible protest against the retreat from the American Dream,
denouncing the wrong culprit as often as the right one.

Jules Chametzky

Reflections on *U. S. A.*
as Novel and Play

The off-Broadway production of *U.S.A.*, "a new dramatic review" written by John Dos Passos and Paul Shyre and based on Dos Passos' novel, has been running in the theatre of New York's Hotel Martinique for several months, so that it seems to have won popular acceptance along with the critical praise that greeted its appearance. I am more than usually interested in this fact, since I recently taught Dos Passos' novel and found that its reception by intelligent students nurtured in the Eisenhower years was an equivocal and conditioned one. To be crude about it, my students responded to the technique of the novel, not to its content; after seeing the dramatization based on it, I wonder if the same—or worse—may not be true of the contemporary theatre audience. "Worse" because it seems to me that in this production the aspect of communion and revelation which the theatrical experience always contains, intensified in this instance by the technically brilliant sense of immediacy evoked, is in the service of a content that is only superficially and momentarily challenging, disturbing, *felt*. The production is, finally, the occasion for a species of audience self-congratulation.

Reflecting upon these conclusions—and, no doubt, in coming to them—I am led back to my recent experience with the novel. I assigned the book in a seminar on "problems" in American literature and language. The "problem" set for the course was recognizably academic—"The Writer and Society"—but, as it developed, the literature we concentrated on—American literature in the 1930's—often made the class crackle with excitement. At times one could almost imagine that a decade or two did not matter: a few mornings a week there was the possibility of recreating a passionate intellectual atmosphere—if not of a cafeteria on 14th Street, then at least of what a college classroom in the era of FDR might have been like. Almost, but not quite. For we were at the end of the 50's, and many of the issues of the 30's were (happily) dead and academic, many of the

Reprinted from *The Massachusetts Review*, I (Winter, 1960), 391-99, by permission of the Massachusetts Review, Inc. © 1960 The Massachusetts Review, Inc.

formerly stirring appeals and heroic postures caused only polite embarrassment, and—most unnerving to a teacher—there was too often only the student's blank incomprehension.

This last was the group's initial response to *U.S.A.*, a book that I thought should hit them like a bombshell. After all, had not a college generation seen in the book, as Harry Levin has observed, a "putting together what seemed to be the contradictions of the world we were growing into"? Had not trustees objected, careers been threatened, when *The Big Money* was taught at the University of Texas not too long ago? In my class of sophisticated undergraduate and graduate students in the academic year 1959–1960, however, the novel threatened to be a dud. It was Dos Passos himself who, very dramatically, saved the situation. The ice was broken when I played for them a tape-recording of a statement Dos Passos had made in 1956 about his methods and purposes in writing *U.S.A.* Because it is such an effective statement and of value to anyone interested in the work of Dos Passos as well as to the course of these reflections, I shall here reproduce the full text:

> When I started *Manhattan Transfer* thirty or more years ago, my aim was to contrive a highly energized sort of novel. I wanted to find some way of making the narrative carry a very large load. Instead of far away and long ago, I wanted it to be here and now. A good deal of the French and Italian writing that fell into my hands while I was serving in the Ambulance service during the first of the great wars, was headed in the same direction. The Italian futurists, the Frenchmen of the school of Rimbaud, the scraps of verse of the poets who went along with cubism, in painting, were trying to do something that stood up off the page. "Simultaneity," they called it.
>
> Of course, I'd been very much affected by the sort of novel Stendhal originated in French with his *Chartreuse de Parme* and Thackeray in English with *Vanity Fair*. I remember reading *Vanity Fair* for the tenth time rather early in my life. After that I lost count. It was the sort of novel in which the story is really a pretext for the presentation of the slice of history the novelist has seen enacted before his own eyes. The personal adventures keep merging with the social chronicle. Historic events, dimly imagined, misunderstood, incompletely envisioned, take the place of the Olympians of the ancient drama. I read James Joyce's *Ulysses* a little later, on my way home from Europe with a bad case of flu, in a tiny inside cabin on one of the big English liners. It got linked in my mind with Sterne's *Tristram Shandy*. Sterne, too, was trying to make his narrative carry a very large load. I had for some time been taken with the meticulous discipline of Defoe's narrative, and Fielding's and Smollett's rollicking satire. But I have to admit that

Fielding and Smollett really came to me through old Captain Marryat's sea stories that gave me infinite pleasure when I was a small boy.

I began with using whatever I had learned from all these methods to produce a satirical chronicle of the world I knew. I felt that everything should go in—popular songs, political aspirations and prejudices, ideals, delusions, clippings out of old newspapers. The raw material of this sort of fiction is everything you've seen and heard and felt—your childhood, your education, serving in the army, and travelling in odd places and finding yourself in odd situations. It's those rare moments of suffering and delight when a man's private sensations are amplified and illuminated by a flash of insight that give him the certainty that what he is seeing and feeling is what millions of his fellow-men see and feel in the same situation. This sort of universal experience is the raw material of all the imaginative arts. These flashes of insight, when strong emotions key all the perceptions up to their highest point, are the nuggets of pure gold. They are rare, even in the lives of the greatest poets.

The novelist has to use all the stories people tell about themselves, all the little dramas in other people's lives he gets glimpses of without knowing just what went before of just what will come after, the fragments of talk he overhears on a subway or on a streetcar, the letter he picks up on the street addressed by one unknown character to another, the words on a scrap of paper found in a trashbasket, the occasional vistas of reality that flash from the mechanical diction of newspaper reports—these are the raw materials the chronicles of your own time are made up of. No matter how much leg-work you do, you can't see it all yourself. You're dealing with scraps and fragments. A lot of it has to be second-hand. The fictional imagination depends on being able to reconstruct the whole unseen animal from a tooth and a toenail and a splinter of skull. Of course sometimes you go wrong, like the anthropologists who fell for Piltdown man.

It was that sort of impulse that produced the three *U.S.A.* novels. Somewhere along the line I'd been impressed by Eisenstein's contrived documentaries, such as *Potemkin.* "Montage" was the word used in those days to describe the juxtaposition of contrasting scenes in motion pictures. I took to montage to try to make the narrative stand up off the page. In the next set of the *District of Columbia* novels, I was trying to fuse the whole thing into a single flow of narrative, with more emphasis on the satirical intent. In *Chosen Country* I tried to make the current of the narrative even more dense, in an elegiac mode very different from the continual present-tense of *Manhattan Transfer* and *U.S.A.* And so it goes.

Here was enough material for discussion during a month of Tuesdays, Thursdays, and Saturdays. What happened in my group was this: when they heard Dos Passos, who had been invited to comment on the content *and* technique of *U.S.A.*, speak so fully—and almost exclusively—about the technical problems he had faced and the means he had used to solve these problems, they relaxed, their responses thawed, they "understood" Dos Passos and his book. The interrelationship of the juxtaposed narrative, Biographies, Newsreels, Camera Eye now could be charted with a "shock of recognition" and pleasure as each element did its work of commenting upon, paralleling, bridging, foreshadowing, underscoring the others. To these close and agile readers, the class war emerged only as a convenient structural device organizing the various stories of the haves and the have-nots (and, incidentally, earning Dos Passos a demerit for his lack of complexity). The motif of failure was bound up with the formal effort to write "a satirical chronicle." *U.S.A.* was primarily significant as the contrivance of "a highly energized sort of novel." The montage technique was brilliantly effective in achieving this end; and insofar as it did, the work was alive, it was not "far away and long ago, . . . [but] here and now." And my heart sank.

For, finally, in this technique of reading, the only ground of response seemed to be the perception of lesser or greater patterning, control, self-containment. Only in this way was *U.S.A.* apparently adaptable, to the "here and now": that is, before it could come alive for students today the bitterness of the controlling social vision that filled the book had to be drained.

Now I am not urging the notion that "meaning" exists apart from formal and aesthetic considerations; I *am* disturbed, however, by the absorption in technique alone, as the means and end of a work of art. Meaning and form are inconceivable apart from each other—this is a truism, yet it merits ceaseless repetition. And in *U.S.A.* technique is wholly integrated with and at the service of a forceful expression about society. Despite my students' absorption in the mechanics of expression, despite the introductory lyric in the book that tells us *U.S.A.* is "mostly the speech of the people," despite Dos Passos' avoidance in his broadcast of the ideological content of his novel, *U.S.A.* is more than just "a highly energized sort of novel." The book fairly shrieks at us its "message"; *U.S.A.* is jangling headlines; public and private banalities; corruption in speech, thought, action; histories of lives of tragic desperation, betrayal, martyrdom, futility, bitterness. When the stories of failure and defeat at every turn in the novel—Centralia, and Veblen, and Debs, and (most crucially) Sacco-Vanzetti—are to be "saved" from being "dated" by seeing them as pieces in a formal and abstract mosaic rather than at the center of the book, it is a hollow victory. If this *is* the price we have to pay in order to read the book today, then perhaps we would be better off to recognize that *U.S.A.* is dated and relegate it to its proper place in some historical limbo. Otherwise, while no one in his right mind would call *U.S.A.* a "happy" book, it surely cannot be confronted in the way that it has a right to be: wholly, and as, in Alfred Kazin's judgment, "one of the saddest books ever written by an American."

The play at the Martinique is by no means a sad one, a fact which, as a paying customer, I will admit to be pure gain; yet, from another standpoint, this may represent a loss. The sadness—or bitterness—in the novel had the power to inform and transform; the play—which as the program notes, is only "based" on the novel—strikes an occasional sombre note that promises to penetrate to the heart, but these turn out to be only titillations, and the object has been only entertainment, after all.

Let me say at once that the production is excellent and, I would guess, superior to almost anything on Broadway this season. The virtuosity of the actors, writers, and director in fashioning a smooth-flowing continuous action that embodies a recognizable point-of-view is remarkable. In view of this, one soon abandons the skeptical idea that so panoramic a novel cannot be adapted to the dimensions of an evening's drama. Mr. Shyre proves once again that through a daring use of theatrical resources requiring only mind and talent, very little is outside the province of theatre. Our audiences are ready for almost anything, technically. On the other hand, there is a good deal lost in the transition from the novel (as I read it) to the play. What I should like to suggest is that this loss is due less to the requirements of the dramatic form than to the demands of the "here and now"—in this case, to the real or supposed expectations of the well-dressed, well-cushioned, well-coifed audience that helps the play keep going. The reduction—especially the excision of almost everything "radical" (Debs is kept: the image of the saint deserted by the workers)—may also reflect Dos Passos' own changed social philosophy.

The setting is simple, geared to the work's demand for fluidity. The audience is seated on three sides of a small theatre; the fourth wall is covered with a large yellow backdrop on which is sketched a jagged mural suggesting aspects of the years between 1900 and 1930. Six wire-backed high stools are placed against this wall for the actors—three men and three women. From here the actors step forward to play their various parts in the narratives (the props down front are reduced to essentials: several chairs, a table or two), chant the headlines of the Newsreel portions, or address the audience directly in the Biography and Camera Eye sections. This is no concert reading, such as Mr. Shyre has successfully prepared with the work of O'Casey: the overall result represents a successful synthesis of Living Newspaper techniques, Epic theatre, a variety show, a review. The production is exciting.

Unfortunately, I do not feel that the content of the play and the conception behind it evenly fulfill the high expectations generated by its technical excellence. While the play was in rehearsal I have been told, Dos Passos reminded the actors that scenes are like icebergs and that they must always be aware of all that does not show. With the exception of some memorable moments, however, I had the uncomfortable feeling that I was seeing an inverted iceberg—almost everything *was* surface—the sense of depth was missing. This was perhaps due to the unrelieved sense of the actors "playing" their parts. The frequency of change in person and situation tended to force the actors into stock mannerisms in order to convey quickly a character and mood, so that the portrayals were too often caricatures. As a way of forcing the audience to achieve an ironic detachment and cool intellectuality towards the characters this is commendable, but the objects of our deliberation must be complex enough to justify the effort. Where the range of irony is limited, where, for example, only a few examples of spurious attitudes and personalities are isolated from the richness and complexity of the novel, the technique wears a little thin. We are repeatedly urged to consider the same absurdities—self-importance, self-infatuation, mindless reliance on cant and jargon, hypocrisy—until, finally, their concrete embodiments are only illustrations, not realities. And when the satirical treatment of these "humors" is not too general, it goes off in search of dead or dying horses.

By heavily underlining the inane aspects of the popular and official culture, the Newsreel portions attempt to locate these absurdities in the society as a whole. But soon the play of voices takes on a pattern: the politicians all begin to sound like Senator Claghorn; the sole radical demonstrator in the play is given a comically whining Brooklyn accent; Gertrude Ederle lumbers down to deliver her headlines in a tough male voice. The actress who plays Gertrude gets a deserved laugh as she bangs the water from her ear, but too much of this sort of thing has the effect, finally, of reducing the whole social scene to a kind of cartoon. The audience laughs, and is comfortably assured that there can be no connection between them and *them*. It's all good clean fun. And nice to be reminded how we've outgrown those dear, dead days of long ago—and the funny clothes, and the funny dances.

The chief burden of the play is carried in the stories of Janey Williams, J. Ward Moorehouse, and Richard Ellsworth Savage. The problem is not that *everyone* in the novel could not be in the play; the problem is, why these three? They each begin as touching or promising people, and each becomes, in one way or another, hollow, corrupt, opportunistic. Although individual corruption is surely an important aspect of the thematic structure in the novel, the play lacks the corrosive effect of a whole society hell-bent on the big money and futility. Of course, Morehouse and Savage occupy positions of power in society and are not merely its victims, so that as products and carriers of our society's illness they could be doubly ominous. But the actors have such fun making fun of these self-evidently absurd characters that the threat to our composure they might represent is minimized. The iceberg does not seem so deep or so treacherous. It seems significant that the people selected for sharp focus are in the public relations game. Morehouse and Savage are early Madison Avenue—which may be an effective symbol of general emptiness at that, but the rest of us *know* we're not Madison Avenue, so that as an all-inclusive symbol it is bound to fail. The play ends with Dick Savage settling smugly and cynically into his new role as a titan in the field. I suppose that is the "message" for the "here and now"—here is the menace in American life. This is certainly part of the truth—but it is such a *fashionable* thing to attack.

Greater depths are hinted at in the play: the wonderfully comic World War I private soldier—an American Schweik—bombarded on all sides by voices filling the air with platitudes and patriotic slogans, plaintively asking, "Can't anyone tell me how to get back to my outfit?"; the unutterably sad scenes between Joe and Janey Williams amidst the shabby-genteel pretensions of Georgetown; the savage irony in the passages dealing with the selection of an Unknown Soldier. The raw bitterness is occasionally there—the play still says more than most contemporary works—but for the most part it serves as a counterpoint, teasing the imagination.

The emphasis in the Biographies is necessarily selective and interestingly slanted. Five biographies are offered: the Wright Brothers, Debs, Valentino, Henry Ford, Isidora Duncan. Isidora's portrait is last and receives the fullest and most "dramatic" treatment, as if it were intended to be the symbolic center of the play. The note that a society is hostile to its most sensitive people is certainly a serious one and should be sounded clearly and unambiguously, to lodge implacably in our minds and hearts and do its transforming work. But here, too, the effect is muffled: Isidora, after all, was terribly eccentric (and who can say she was driven to it by our hostility?), and her mode of life too remote to make a full assault upon the audience's sensibilities. Everyone knows we have treated an occasional artist shabbily—but times have changed, and besides, Isidora had her glory.

I think there are Biographies in the book, and stories, that would lie upon us like open wounds, but they were not done. Instead, a narrator reminds us at the close of the play that "U.S.A. is the lives of its people,"—forgetful of all those who did not receive a hearing—and smiles at us. We smile back. The lights go up; the playing is over.

John H. Wrenn

"U. S. A."

I   A Book of Memories

U.S.A. is first of all a book of memories. These memories, all relating to the United States during the first third of the twentieth century, are presented and developed contrapuntally in autobiography, history, biography, and fiction. The form is that of the associational process of memory itself, by which perceptions are established in the mind and later recalled. And the purpose of the work is equivalent to the function of the memory: to establish in the mind perceptions which, in association with other perceptions from experience such as those of pleasure or pain, develop into attitudes toward certain kinds of experience, frames of reference, or standards by which we judge today.

Dos Passos' intent was to establish for himself and his audience a broad and pertinent framework of memory. This required a maximum selective recall of his own experience, supplemented by the general experience and that of other individuals recorded in documents of the times. It also required an imaginative organization of these materials into a mnemonic unity which could suggest appro-

Reprinted from John H. Wrenn, *John Dos Passos* (New York: Twayne Publishers, 1961), pp. 154-66, by permission of Twayne Publishers, Inc. Copyright 1961 by Twayne Publishers, Inc.

priate attitudes toward related kinds of past, present, and future experience.

If he could get a sequence of enough memories, or even a characteristic segment of them, into focus in his camera's eye, he could develop it, edit it, and give it artistic form. Then he could run it through again, stop the motion for a moment if he wished, and present a close-up or a flash-back: "Now who was that, could that have been me in that funny hat?" He could also give a tune or a speech on the sound track. The viewer might even leave the theater wiser than when he went in; at any rate, a few people might risk a nickel to see it. It would probably be misleadingly advertised as one of the "exclusive presentations of the Mesmer Agency" containing comments on "the great and near great" and "a fund of racy anecdotes"— as Dos Passos later satirized the bally-hooing of his books in *The Prospect Before Us* (1950). But for himself, he would present it only as one man's attempt "to add his nickel's worth."

When it was ready, some risked their nickels; and almost the first thing they saw was the producer-director as a little child flitting across the screen, like Alfred Hitchcock sneaking into his own films. As autobiography Dos Passos presented his own story directly in the Camera Eye sequences, in stream-of-consciousness—or more accurately, stream-of-memory—narration. His story in *The 42nd Parallel* is almost entirely separate from the rest of his history of the country in the early years of the century; but, as the novel progresses through the three volumes, there is a continuous tightening in the relationship of its several parts—narrative, Camera Eyes, Newsreels, biographies—as the narrator becomes one with his subject.

In *1919* the autobiography of the Camera Eyes begins to merge with the fictional story of Dick Savage, especially at Harvard and in the war. Toward the end of the final volume, *The Big Money*, Camera Eyes Forty-nine and Fifty include indirect biography of Sacco and Vanzetti; and in between those two sequences Dos Passos' story merges with the fictional story of Mary French in her work for the Sacco-Vanzetti defense and with the history of the time as outlined in Newsreel LXVI. Finally, within the last twenty-five pages of the trilogy, the fictional Ben Compton (the prototype of Glenn Spottswood in his next novel, *Adventures* and of Jay Pignatelli in *Chosen Country*), expresses, peering "through his thick glasses," Dos Passos' relationship to the Communist Party: "oppositionist . . . exceptionalism . . . a lot of nonsense." And in the final sketch, "Vag," of the last two and a half pages, the Camera Eye has become the biography of the depression vagrant, a distinctive phenomenon of the times. It is also very nearly the picture of Jimmy Herf hitchhiking west out of Manhattan.

In *U.S.A.* Dos Passos placed himself securely within the history of his country in his time. But he emphasized the history above the importance of his relation to it. As an historian, he did not need to be told that his country's own brand of idealism was "democracy"; the problem was to discover what the word meant. It seemed to have pretty much lost its meaning at about the time the United States had fought a war to make the world safe for it. Taking the word at its pre-war value, Dos Passos devoted his trilogy to a history of the struggle for industrial democracy in America.

As a critic Dos Passos has always been principally interested in the effects of phenomena upon individual men and women. This interest helped to make him a novelist; and it—and not simply his training as a novelist—focuses all of his histories upon personalities and traits of character. The focus of *U.S.A.,* therefore, is upon the twenty-six *actual* persons engaged in the struggle and the twelve principal *fictional* persons also engaged in it and affected by it. The actual people of the biographies are those who influenced the pattern of the struggle—labor leaders, politicians, artists, journalists, scientists, and business leaders. The fictional characters represent average men and women molded by the complex forces about them.

The fictional characters illustrate more than anything else the dissolution of the once central cohesive institution in American society (the one Dos Passos first achieved with his marriage in 1929, as he began *U.S.A.*), the family. Although most of them come from fairly secure family units, they are unable to form them for themselves. The fictional narrative is filled with pathetic promiscuity, perversion, vague temporary alliances, divorces, abortions. Ben Compton, again, sums up the need at the end of *The Big Money.* Speaking to Mary French, who is one of the most sympathetically portrayed of the principal characters and whose maternal instincts have made her a devoted worker for the oppressed, Ben says, "You know if we hadn't been fools we'd have had that baby that time . . . we'd still love each other."

In Dos Passos' picture of the U.S.A., it was essential to reinstitute the family; but neither of the two larger institutions in which the forces of the times had become polarized—*laissez-faire* capitalism and Stalinist communism—appeared to permit its free growth. Until people achieved a social system which would give the average man a sense of participation—of responsibility for and pride in his work—the smaller, more vital social units would be ineffective. To achieve that system, the meaning of the old mercantile-agrarian democracy and its libertarian phraseology—liberty, equality, pursuit of happiness—must somehow be restored in the scientific, urban-industrial present.

The makers of that present and those who hoped to remake it are the subjects of the biographies. Toward each of the principal fictional characters, each of whom is seen as a child, the reader shares Dos Passos' affection, which turns to scorn or pity as they become mere cogs or pulp in the capitalist or communist machines, or to indignation as their individualism leaves them crushed and dead—like Joe Williams and Daughter, both killed by accident in France in the aftermath of the war—or stranded and alone like Ben Compton. Toward the biographies, however, the reader's reaction is principally a sharing of the burning indignation with which most of them were written. Of the twenty-six, not counting the two portraits of the anonymous Unknown Soldier and "Vag," fourteen are sympathetic and twelve are not.

The criterion of judgment of them as of the fictional characters is the courage or will of the individual to maintain the faith that most of them were born to in the untarnished meanings of the democratic creed. By this criterion we recognize them as friends or strangers whatever their births or origins or ends. If their work is intended to uphold the dignity of the individual man and woman and the integrity of their language as Americans, they are friends. If they are scornful or even like Edison and Henry Ford merely "unconcerned with the results of (their) work in human terms," they are the "strangers" of Camera Eye Fifty, "who have turned our language inside out who have taken the clean words our fathers spoke and made them slimy and foul."

Dos Passos is not all mysterious as to his purposes; he even states them directly in Camera Eyes Forty-seven and Forty-nine of *The Big Money:* ". . . shape words remembered light and dark straining to rebuild yesterday to clip out paper figures to stimulate growth Warp newsprint into faces smoothing and wrinkling in the various barelyfelt velocities of time." Or again, reporting his reporting of the Sacco-Vanzetti case: "pencil scrawls in my notebook the scraps of recollection the broken halfphrases the effort to intersect word with word to dovetail clause with clause to rebuild out of mangled memories unshakably (Oh Pontius Pilate) the truth." Here is the meaning of the terms "straight writing" and "architect of history."

Yet the architect of history works not only "to rebuild yesterday" as the foundation of today, but to build of today a sound foundation for tomorrow. By straight writing and with the materials of contemporary speech, the writer provides contexts of meaning for today's speech, which will be the basis of tomorrow's memories. Dos Passos achieves his contexts through the use of dialogue and even of direct narration phrased in the colloquial language appropriate to the character he is treating. The reader sees and hears the speech in conjunction with actions and through the consciousness of the character concerned. We participate in the individual's attitudes toward events.

Further than this, Dos Passos has the reader share, at least for the moment, the attitudes of quite different individuals toward the same or similar events. We see the affair between Dick Savage and Daughter (Anne Elizabeth Trent), for instance, through the eyes and feelings of each of them. To Dick it is simply an affair which becomes awkward and threatens to embarrass him in his career when Daughter expects him to feel some responsibility for her pregnancy. To her it is a tremendous event which results in tragedy. The reader also sees and experiences a variety of attitudes toward business, labor, government, the war, the Sacco-Vanzetti case, and many other institutions and particular events. Since he cannot sympathetically entertain at the same time two opposing attitudes toward a single phenomenon, he is forced to choose, to criticize, to formulate standards.

As a realist Dos Passos reveals his characters in the historical framework of time, place, and social milieu which help to form them. These backgrounds, usually presented through the memories of the characters themselves, are various enough to provide a representative cross-section, geographically and socially, of American society. In the "Introduction" to *Three Soldiers,* Dos Passos remarked that "our beds have made us and the acutest action we can take is to sit up on the edge of them and look around and think." In describing his characters' beds, Dos Passos is an objective reporter of existing phenomena. But in portraying the individuals themselves and their attempts to sit up and look around and think, he is a selective critic. He controls our choice of attitude by creating characters with whom we must at first sympathize, for their beds and their wants are ours. We continue to sympathize as they struggle to express themselves and to satisfy their needs; but we become indignant at the Procrustean forces that chain them prone in their beds or at the individuals as they lose the courage to struggle, refuse to think, or prefer to crawl back under the sheets within the security of the familiar narrow limits of their bedsteads.

II Tools of Language

Half of the fictional characters of *U.S.A.* and nearly half of the subjects of the biographies have a special facility with the tools of language, the means with which to build or to restrict human freedom. Of the fictional ones, most are poor or careless keepers of their talents. J. Ward Moorehouse becomes a public-relations executive—a propagandist for big business who exploits language for profit; Janey becomes his expert private secretary and an efficient, warped old maid; Dick Savage degenerates from a young poet to Moorehouse's administrative assistant and contact-man—a sort of commercial pimp. Mac surrenders his principles as an itinerant printer for the labor movement and succumbs to the security offered by a girl and a little bookstore of his own in Mexico; Mary French and Ben Compton become pawns of communist politics. Only Ben emerges at the end, though rejected and alone, still looking around him and thinking.

In contrast, only three of roughly a dozen subjects of the biographies seem to misuse their gifts of language: Bryan, "a silver tongue in a big mouth"; Woodrow Wilson, "talking to save his faith in words, talking . . . talking"; Hearst, whose "empire of the printed word . . . this power over the dreams of the adolescents of the world grows and poisons like a cancer." Most of the heroes of Dos Passos' biographies are chosen from among the heroes and martyrs of the working-class movement: men who looked around, thought critically, and developed their abilities in an effort to restore the meanings rather than to exploit the phraseology of American democracy. They were men like Eugene Debs, Bill Haywood, La Follette, Jack Reed, Randolph Bourne, Paxton Hibben, Joe Hill, Thorstein Veblen.

Dos Passos' own handling of the language can be demonstrated in an example from his fictional narrative in *1919*. Dick Savage at the end of the war is still in Paris; Daughter, spurned by her "Dickyboy" and carrying his child, goes off alone in a taxi; Dick, now captain but angling for a public relations job after the war, goes to bed with a hangover; but he cannot get to sleep:

> Gradually he got warmer. Tomorrow. Seventhirty: shave, buckle puttees. . . . Day dragged out in khaki. . . . Dragged out khaki days until after the signing of the peace. Dun, drab, khaki. Poor Dick got to go to work after the signing of the peace. Poor Tom's cold. Poor Dickyboy . . . Richard . . . He brought his feet up to where he could rub them. Poor Richard's feet. After the signing of the Peace.

Dick is a Harvard graduate; he had intended to become a writer. He has nearly lost our sympathy because of his attitude toward

Daughter. Here he gives up the struggle to sit up and think as he climbs literally and figuratively into bed, self-indulgent, self-pitying. "Poor Tom" suggests his subconscious awareness of his disguise—in part the uniform of an officer and a gentleman, in part his role of a dedicated poet; and it also suggests the contrast of his character with that of Edgar in *King Lear*. "Poor Dickeyboy" reveals the transfer of his pangs of conscience into self-sympathy. "Poor Richard" indicates his falling from critical awareness into the thoughtless selfishness of the old American cliché of success (Franklin's Poor Richard and Horatio Alger's Ragged Dick), as he resumes the foetal position because he lacks the courage to think and to doubt; he has, in the vernacular, cold feet: "By the time his feet were warm he'd fallen asleep."

The picture is at once comic and pathetic and somewhat revolting. Up to about this point we have been sympathizing with Dick as another struggling, wanting human; suffering with him; and enjoying his occasional successes as our own. In this passage, Dos Passos' method prevents our suddenly ceasing to participate. We must share Dick's experience—after all a rather ordinary one, already familiar to us—at the same time that we reject it. We share from within his consciousness; we observe and reject from outside it. By the multiplication of such experiences Dos Passos attempts to establish in the reader something like what T. S. Eliot called the objective correlative of the work of art; but another name for it is a critical standard or part of a frame of reference. Once established, it exists outside of, even independent of, its original source. If Dick Savage's retreat from responsibility, for example, is established as symbolic of all retreat from responsibility, and if we are made to reject it here, then we must reject it whenever we encounter it.

This process Dos Passos once explained in a little-known "Introductory Note" to the first Modern Library edition of his *42nd Parallel* as the destruction and reconstruction of stereotypes. He was aware that it would probably lose him readers: "People feel pain when the stereotype is broken, at least at first." But it was the necessary method of the architect of history. The reaction from the reader is similar to the "grin of pain" that Dos Passos described as the essential response to satire in his essay about George Grosz in 1936.

Yet the reader's reaction to Dos Passos' novels is only remotely and occasionally one of mirth. To *U.S.A.* it is more nearly a grim realization of the sores and weaknesses of our culture which cry out for repair. To some readers, doubtless, it is too bad that Dos Passos is not more nearly the satirist than he is. Perhaps a leavening of humor that could change a grimace to a grin would make him more palatable to both readers and critics and, therefore, presumably more effective because more widely read. But Dos Passos' intent is vitally serious. He does not write to entertain but to communicate, to inform—in brief, to educate. He has always been too close to his materials, too involved personally, to be able to attain the special kind of detachment demanded of the satirist. Like Swift indeed, he heartily loves John, Peter, Thomas, and so forth; but he can by no means manage a principal hate and detestation for that animal called man.

III   Method of Tragedy

Rather than satire—or rather including the satire and including also his naturalism—Dos Passos' method in *U.S.A.* is that of tragedy, a method based on an ironic attitude toward the past. *U.S.A.* is a great agglomerate tragic history. The protagonist, obviously enough, is the real U.S.A. in the first third of the twentieth century. Its tragic characters are the real subjects of the biographies: Debs, Luther Burbank, Bill Haywood, Bryan, Minor Keith, Carnegie, Edison, Steinmetz, La Follette, Jack Reed, Randolph Bourne, T. R., Paxton Hibben, Woodrow Wilson, and the rest. Merely to read their names is to sense the tragedy of their era: so much talent, ambition, love—all frustrated or misdirected or drained away into war, profits, prohibitions, intolerances, and oppressions.

In the background of the novel, democratic individualism and reliance on the future (pursuit of happiness) are the characteristics which gave U.S.A. its greatness. A too narrow individualism, a too great reliance on the future—a loss of memory—and a warped interpretation of happiness in purely material terms: these are the characteristics which brought on its apparent downfall in the years Dos Passos wrote of. They are the tragic flaws of the society which rejects its best men. But its failures and its worst men have their own equivalent flaws—Bryan's "silver tongue in a big mouth," Wilson's "faith in words," and the overweening ambition of the Morgans, Insull, and others.

The fictional characters—like the anonymous "Vag" and the Unknown Soldier and the narrator—have not the stature of tragic characters. They are the extras, the *demos* or ordinary citizens like ourselves, or the members of the chorus with whom we can participate as they work and suffer in the shadow of the struggle for industrial democracy. Yet, while we participate, we also watch; and for our capacity as objective audience, there is the more formal chorus of the Newsreels, in which the past provides its own ironic commentary about the past and reveals our recent idiocies to ourselves.

Many Americans in the audience have been unwilling to sit through Dos Passos' documentary tragedy. If they have come to it for entertainment or escape, they have been disappointed. But those who have stayed to see and hear have been exposed to a unique dramatic experience. This experience is one of participating satire; for, as Dos Passos said of the painter Grosz, he "makes you identify yourself with the sordid and pitiful object." This identification, in turn, provides the catharsis, "a release from hatred"—in part because the reader or spectator cannot wholly hate himself and in part because the hatred is already expressed more adequately than most could express it through vitriolic portraits of the villains, real and fictional. The uniqueness, however, is in the partial nature of the catharsis: it might be said to be both catharsis and anti-catharsis. The reader is purged only of the self-indulgent emotions of hatred and self-love, which allow him to forget. He is denied complacency and forced to remember. The tragedy he has witnessed is that of the unfulfilled potential of the individual, including himself, in a society dedicated, ironically, to the possibilities of its fulfillment. He is left with a feeling of incompleteness.

Part of the reason for Dos Passos' unpopularity is probably his lack of sufficient self-esteem for the reader to share. His contemporary, Hemingway, for example, had it both in himself and in his characters. Even in Swift the reader can climb to the heights of satire with the author—Gulliver being only an alter ego, the equivalent of some of the fictional characters of *U.S.A.*—and look down on the puny mass of men with the possibility of self-gratulation that he is not among them. But in Dos Passos' participating satire even the author is satirized; if the reader indulges in any identification (which he can scarcely avoid), he must lose not only his self-esteem but also his complacency.

Dos Passos' self-esteem is almost wholly of the abstract "self," the essential *I, you, me, he, she* of the tragically unfulfilled individual potential. In fact, it is almost the sole object of his esteem. So where another writer—and particularly another autobiographical writer such as Hemingway—might appear to caress his characters, possibly because they contain so much of the author, Dos Passos scorns his, partly for the same reason. He scorns them also because they are not true individuals and because it is not his fault, but theirs. He cannot help them; for, if they are to achieve their individuality, to fulfill their potentials, they must do it themselves. The most he can do is to help define the problem and some of the conditions of its solution. Yet Dos Passos is thoroughly sympathetic, especially towards the fictional men and women who give their names to the

narrative sections of *U.S.A.* He shows a pervading pity for his characters, real and fictional, which is evident even in his most acidulous
biographical portraits; an example is his quoting from the pathetically
presumptuous will of the first J. P. Morgan in his biography of "The
House of Morgan" in *1919.*

Both the scorn and the pity come through to the reader. Since
one can properly scorn only inevitable weakness or meanness, the
reader is left at the end of the tragedy with a sense of awe not so
much at the power and authority of the destructive or restricting
external forces as at the potential beauty and unity of the thing
destroyed, the free personality. Bernard De Voto felt it in "the gusto
and delight of American living" whose absence in *U.S.A.* he so deplored.

Yet this sense of incompleteness in the reader—the feeling of having
been cheated of some of the ideal goods of life and that something
should be done about it—is precisely the reaction that Dos Passos,
the architect of history, desired. Unfortunately for his purposes, many
readers have felt only the incompleteness and have missed the further
implications of his criticism that something can be done about it,
but that each individual must do it himself.

IV Doubt and Affirmation

Perhaps one reason for the failure of his message is related to the
fact that he has had one. As a novelist his chief concern has been,
as he wrote in "The Business of a Novelist" for the *New Republic*
in April, 1934, "to create characters first and foremost, and then
to set them in the snarl of the human currents of his time, so that
there results an accurate permanent record of a phase of history."
Yet as a man with a message, his chief concern has been with its
recipients; and his characters, despite the sympathy of his portrayal,
he has left deliberately underdeveloped. Similarly, he has always
aimed at discomforting his readers—at stirring them into fresh
thought and action by destroying the stereotypes from which they
viewed the world. The great antagonist of *U.S.A.* is complacency.
Probably most of the adverse criticism of the novel could be traced,
like De Voto's to the critics' protests against Dos Passos' attack on
one or another of their complacencies. "When complacency goes,"
Dos Passos concluded his critical appreciation of Grosz, "young in-
telligence begins."

The essential first step to the freedom of intelligent action was
to doubt. Yet some compromise between doubt and acceptance must

be made before real action can begin. Until the early thirties Dos Passos' compromise was in the acceptance of immediate goals: in broadening the range of his own experience and in satisfying chiefly through travel his eager curiosity about the world around him; in participating directly in behalf of the obviously oppressed such as Sacco and Vanzetti, the Scottsboro boys, and, later, refugees from Europe; and in endeavoring to stimulate doubt in others. Then sometime before the fall elections of 1936 he reached the climax of his own doubting: his doubt turned inward upon itself.

The struggle of this moral crisis can be read in Camera Eye Forty-six early in *The Big Money:* "if not why not? walking the streets rolling on your bed eyes sting from peeling the speculative onion of doubt if somebody in your head top dog? underdog? didn't (and on Union Square) say liar to you." From this point on, the reader can trace the development of his Everlasting Yea, which begins with his condemnation of both the capitalistic and communistic viewpoints in *The Big Money* and his enthusiastic vote for Roosevelt in 1936 and which culminates in his novel *Chosen Country,* in his appreciative study of Jefferson, and in his two recent histories of the founders of the republic, *The Men Who Made the Nation* (1957) and *Prospects of a Golden Age* (1959).

In his probing into the meanings of the democratic phraseology and their bearings on his country in his time, Dos Passos found what he sought in an appreciation of the dynamics of his society. From his study of the history of his country and his awareness of the forces of history in action—particularly in the increase of despotism abroad—he came to realize that, for him, the U.S.A. *was* the last, best hope of men.

"The shape of a piece of work should be imposed, and in a good piece of work always is imposed, by the matter," Dos Passos wrote in his "Introductory Note" to the first Modern Library edition of *The 42nd Parallel.* The conscious, organized incompleteness of *U.S.A.* was not merely a device to stimulate the reader; it was the artistic form imposed by the organic necessity of the artist's materials. His study of his matter, American history, had finally revealed to him the secret of form in his society: that the pattern of American society lay where he had intuitively recognized it in the individual—in its potential and incompleteness. Sometime during the composition of his trilogy, Dos Passos became aware of a resurgence of what must have been a still-existing fluidity and dynamic potential in the American social structure. In such a society a man, if he would, could give meaning to his life.

Having intellectually grasped the pattern—or at least one which was satisfying and meaningful to him—and realized its form in his art in *U.S.A.,* Dos Passos had accomplished his major task as an artist. His materials for *U.S.A.* were all historical—the products of his study of the nation's past, his awareness of significant events acting about him, and a mass of painfully remembered detail from his own life. By the effort of his imagination, he constructed from these materials an organic unity which revealed the nation which he had made his own. By his own efforts he had carved out his niche and made himself a citizen.

Believing above all in the responsible and purposeful action of the free individual, Dos Passos was not a man to waste in inaction the freedom he had taken forty years to acquire, or to take lightly the duties of citizenship. However, having achieved the form he sought in his life and in his art, his energies could now take a slightly different direction. History in the service of art had completed the pattern. Henceforth Dos Passos' efforts would be more nearly historical than artistic. Art in the service of history should confirm the pattern and maintain the flexibility of the form.

George Knox

Voice in the *U. S. A.* Biographies

Late in the fall of 1959, in the off-Broadway theater, The Martinique, Dos Passos' *U.S.A.* was reincarnated in dramatic performance. Actors in 1920's "costume" read one thread of the trilogy, the J. Ward Moorehouse story, and some of the short biographies, apparently with powerful effect. One is not surprised to hear this, particularly of the short biographies. Dos Passos worked a good deal in the theatre, not only writing plays but designing sets as well, during the twenties. The short biographies interest us particularly here. In *U.S.A.* they serve a structural function similar to the color harmonies in such early works as *One Man's Initiation* and *Three Soldiers*. But color contrast and harmony have given way to personality tones

Reprinted from *Texas Studies in Literature and Language* vol. IV, no. 1 (Spring, 1962), 109-16, by permission of the journal and the author.

and "voices." The effect of these interstitial lives, or biographical asides, is largely aural. We hear with the authorial-listener, who in *U.S.A.* expresses our cultural identity through these representative heroes.

Dos Passos, speaking a kind of divine-average language, a synthesis of Flaubert and Sandburg, links the biographies and the fictional lives "tight by the tendrils of phrased words." Epic bard of barbed words, poetic Veblen, he erects ironic memorials to our cultural identity in the saga of *U.S.A.,* "riveted into the language: the sharp prism of his mind." Amidst the Newsreels, which establish the mass-mind atmosphere, and the Camera Eye, the interior monologue of a sensitive observer, himself a part of the drama, sound the biographies. The newspaper headlines are staccato and cacophonic. The Camera Eye fragments are lyrical, subjective, brooding. The impressionistic portraits are the aural-images most closely tuned to reality, in the sense that they constitute identifiable historical voices. The biographies exemplify, ironically, many of Carlyle's (*Heroes and Hero-Worship*) and Emerson's (*Representative Men*) tenets about the "poetic" nature of biography. Achieving a maximum dramatism, they combine the Carlylean dictum that biography is the true poem and the Emersonian dictum that men have a pictorial or representative quality.

Dos Passos, like his "Luther Burbank," hybridizes forms in an era of form-destroying, the form of art imitating the formlessness of life in the twenties. The three novels are reduced to situations, the plot to scenes, the character to humors and tones. The historical dramatis personae, or "parts," constitute a setting for the fiction, a harmony-in-contrast, seen and heard as they are through the ironic language.

Hence, a vibrant and charged aural dimension exists as the middle-ground between audience and subject, as well as in the background between author and subject, arrested momentarily in the detrital flow of American legendry. Dos Passos effaces contours, working through indirect exposition, speech fragments, vocabulary tics, odd verbal gestures, representative locutions. The "color" of the characters shades into the tones of the authorial conversation with history, which is unfinished, unending.

> . . . it was the speech that clung to the ears, the link that tingled in the blood; U.S.A. . . . U.S.A. is the letters at the end of an address when you are away from home. But mostly U.S.A. is the speech of the people.

The "young man" who anonymously introduces the three volumes appears in the last sketch in *The Big Money,* "Vag." He is a kind of Wolfian-Whitmanesque center-of-consciousness, our lost youth, our innocent wanderer on the road. As we read the introductory sketch we perhaps hear echoes of the voice in Whitman's "The Sleepers":

> I wander all night in my vision,
> Stepping with light feet, swiftly and noiselessly stepping
>   and stopping,
> Bending with open eyes over the shut eyes of sleepers,
> Wandering and confused, lost to myself, ill-assorted,
>   contradictory,
> Pausing, gazing, bending, and stopping.

And now Dos Passos:

> The young man walks by himself, fast but not fast enough, far but not far enough (faces slide out of sight, talk trails into tattered scraps, footsteps tap fainter in alleys); he must catch the last subway, the streetcar, the bus, run up the gangplanks of all the steamboats, register in all the hotels, work in the cities, answer the wantads, learn the trades, take up the jobs, live in all the boardinghouses, sleep in all the beds. One bed is not enough, one life is not enough. At night, head swimming with wants, he walks by himself alone. No job, no woman, no house, no city.

In the biographies, "talk trails into tattered scraps," one of the major devices. The tones are remembered tones, a collage of voices:

> Only the ears busy to catch the speech are not alone; the ears are caught tight, linked tight by the tendrils of phrased words, the turn of a joke, the singsong fade of a story, the gruff fall of a sentence; linking tendrils of speech twine through the city blocks, spread over trucks leaving on their long night runs over roaring highways, whisper down sandy byroads past wornout farms, joining up cities and fillingstations, roadhouses, steamboats, planes groping along airways; words call out on mountains pastures, drift slow down rivers widening to the sea and the hushed beaches.

Recognizing this pervasive quality in *U.S.A.*, we come closer to appreciating the formal propriety of the biographies, a choral background to the voices of the young man of the fictional characters.

All of the portraits are built upon conventional third-person narration, although the use to which Dos Passos puts this convention is sometimes peculiar. The broken quality of the narrative is accentuated in the Cummingsesque irregular line length, unconventional punctuation, and lack of capitalization. Sometimes (as in the sketches of Roosevelt and Bryan) the voice of the subject is indicated in italics. In the portraits of Roosevelt and Bryan we hear passages from their speeches. Sometimes the speaker's voice is implied in indirect discourse which is actually the author speaking. In the portrait of Veblen, we hear a "public" voice which often merges with authorial voice to reinforce the desired feeling of disapproval or approval. Direct dramatic dialogue occurs occasionally, as in "Paul Bunyan," where Everest talks with the mob who attack him and kill him. Again, the subject's voice may be used in ballad fashion, as in refrain. "The Body of an American" offers an excellent example of this: *"And there's a hundred million others like me,"* and "Say feller tell me how I can get back to my outfit," or "Say buddy can't you tell me how I can get back to my outfit?" Finally, "Say soldier for chrissake can't you tell me how I can get back to my outfit?" These entries of subject-voice assume a cumulative force, as in the incremental repetition of lines in the ballad, even though they be separated by one or more paragraphs of other textual material.

Dos Passos uses the incremental repetition technique for several effects. First, he is dealing impressionistically with each person. What is it about that person's life that he wishes to accent? Having selected this factor, he will make it a motif by repeating it. Sometimes such a factor is a statement that person made; or it is the peculiarity of some action. That is, Dos Passos essentializes character through isolating some feature and by repetition making it a "tic." Often we find this in a quoted remark, sometimes in italicized intrusion by the author himself, sometimes in a repeated opinion of the populace. In "Fighting Bob," we find "He was one of 'the little group of willful men expressing no opinion but their own'" repeated crucially at the end:

> a stumpy man with a lined face, one leg stuck out in the aisle and
> his arms folded and a chewed cigar in the corner of his mouth
> and an undelivered speech on his desk,
> a willful man expressing no opinion but his own.

Thus, Dos Passos accents a person's ruling passion, his dominant mood, his prevailing humor, or the consistency of a public reaction.

Dos Passos does not often intrude overt evaluative statements, although his bias is usually obvious enough through innuendo, tonal intensification, and irony. Often, he asks at the end of the selection

some question that needs no answer. It contains the answer and
a built-in judgment. The portrait of Minor C. Keith, superimposed
on the fictional career of J. Ward Moorehouse and amidst the minor
swirl of little people struggling business, ends this way:

> Why that uneasy look under the eyes, in the picture of Minor C.
> Keith the pioneer of the fruittrade, the railroad-builder, in all the
> pictures the newspapers carried of him when he died?

Endings are particularly important in the portraits. Often the
ending is diminuendo, trailing off into anticlimax for ironic effect.
Sometimes the whiplash ending achieves its effect through mock
concession to opinion hostile to the subject. Again, Dos Passos em-
ploys the barbed ending through implied quotation, the echo of a
previously repeated direct quotation, from a hostile opponent. A
poemlike ending can also embody a final pronouncement, benediction,
or malediction. Such is the ending to "The House of Morgan" in
1919:

> (Wars and panics on the stock exchange,
> machinegunfire and arson,
> bankruptcies, warloans,
> starvation, lice, cholera and typhus:
> good growing weather for the House of Morgan.)

The distaste for the Morgan financial operations can be contrasted
with the neutral-pose which ends "Joe Hill" in *1919*.

> They put him in a black suit, put a stiff color around his neck and
> a bow tie, shipped him to chicago for a bangup funeral, and pho-
> tographed his handsome stony mask staring into the future.
> The first of May they scattered his ashes to the wind.

Or, the ending is an ironic understatement ("The Body of an American"), the dying-fall, or diminuendo for the trailing-off into futility
("The American Plan" and "Tin Lizzie"). We find also the double-
ending, as in the portrait of Thorstein Veblen ("The Bitter Drink"),
a last request in italics followed by the author's own tribute. Then,
there is the ironic anecdote for ending, as in "Art and Isadora." We
also find an example of imitative form in the soaring ending to the
portrait of the Wright brothers, an ending of positive force.

Most of the portraits utilize parentheses for varied effects. Usually,
the parentheses serve for authorial aside, as Dos Passos takes a

position of omniscient observer situated above the drama as narrated. In addition to the parentheses enclosing authorial interpolation, he (as in "The Boy Orator of the Platte") inserts repeated extracts from public statements in order to give the portrait depth and to create an illusion of massive force. Group and "class" opinion is echoed in parentheses, echoes which give the portraits a dialectical dramatism, indicating oppositions between the subject portrayed and the society or segment of society in which the subject acted. He makes use of italicized passages to intensify the dramatic impact. For one thing, he injects extracts from speeches ("Meester Veelson," "The Boy Orator," "The Happy Warrior") for accretive, incremental build-up of tone. Sometimes the public statement is found in lower-case fine print and in upper-case italics ("The Body of an American"). The portrait can end with an italicized statement by the subject, in most cases for irony. He may also interject passages from newspapers ("Adagio Dancer"), and other "documentary" materials, such as telegrams and letters, in italics.

Throughout the trilogy we notice some similarities to Carlylean harangue, as in *The French Revolution,* but more modern stylistic analogues suggest themselves, particularly cinematic techniques. *U.S.A.* as a whole is constructed in the fashion of a panoramic movie, the Hollywood epic, although no derogation of *U.S.A.* is intended in this parallel. The "Newsreel" and "Camera Eye" passages need no detailed explanation to show such correspondence in style. The portraits themselves are perhaps like movie shorts; or, better, documentary film; or "The March of Time" style of exposition. Fluidity of form is primary. Dos Passos tries to establish a sense of background and foreground simultaneously, as when the speeches of Roosevelt, Bryan, Wilson, Wright, *et al,* intrude in the flow of events. We also get the impression of temporally distinct events concurrently.

The portrait of Paxton Hibben, "A Hoosier Quixote," illustrates some of these features very well. It begins with an extract from the 1928–1929 *Who's Who.* In small italics we get the most fragmentary, neutral, statistical portrayal of a "life," ending with *"A.M. Harvard 1904."* Next, we are projected into a historical context: "Thinking men were worried in the Middle West in the years Hibben was growing up there." And so the narrator fills in the milieu and recreates the cultural background from the barren entries of *Who's Who.* After about eighteen lines we come back to the "actor," Paxton Hibben, as a boy. To move from boyhood to the diplomatic service takes Dos Passos another eighteen lines. There he intrudes another italicized fragment from the *Who's Who* record, carrying him up to the time of retirement. The anticlimatic, cold impersonality of these passages breaks our mood abruptly, whereas the more casual exposition in which they are embedded expands, exhumes, so to speak, the humanity of the subject. We begin to feel through contrast the drama that lies cold in the mere statistics: "3rd sec and 2nd sec American Embassy St. Petersburg and Mexico City 1905-6" is taken up in the next passage thus: "Pushkin for de Musset; St. Petersburg was a young dude's romance . . . "

Once launched into the life, once having given the obituary skeleton some warm flesh, we flashback for kaleidoscopic effect, for crescendo:

> goldencrusted spires under a platinum sky,
> the icegray Neva flowing swift and deep under bridges that jingled with sleighbells;
> riding home from the Islands with the Grand Duke's mistress, the most beautiful most amorous singer of Neapolitan streetsongs;
> Staking a pile of rubies in a tall room glittering with chandeliers, monocles, diamonds dripped on white shoulders;
> White snow, white tableclothes, white sheets,
> Kakhetian wine, Vodka fresh as newmown hay, Astrakhan caviar, sturgeon, Finnish salmon, Lapland ptarmigan, and the most beautiful women in the world;
> but it was 1905, Hibben left the Embassy one night and saw a flare of red against the trampled snow of the Nevsky
> and red flags,
> blood frozen in the ruts, blood trinkling down the cartracks;
> he saw the machineguns on the balconies of the Winter Palace, and Cossacks charging the unarmed crowds that wanted peace and food and a little freedom,
> heard the throaty roar of the Russian Marseillaise; revolt, he walked the streets all night with the revolutionists, got in wrong at the Embassy
> and was transferred to Mexico City where there was no revolution yet, only peons and priests and the stillness of the great volcanoes.

And so the sketch progresses, alternating passages of dramatic acceleration, things seen, comments, breaks—in true Carlylean fashion. The contrast between the mere record in fragmentary intrusions, and the compelling excitement of the narrator's mood builds our own excitement and creates a paradoxical impression of historical urgency and timelessness, something sadly happened and gone. This is film realism, the moment held in closeup while the historical flow moves in the background:

> In Paris they were still haggling over the price of blood, squabbling over toy flags, the river frontiers on reliefmaps, the historical destiny

of peoples, while behind the scenes the good contractplayers, the De-
terdings, the Zahkaroffs, the Stinnesses sat quiet and possessed themselves of the raw materials.

In Moscow there was order,
In Moscow there was work,
In Moscow there was hope;

the *Marseillaise* of 1905, *Onward, Christian Soldiers* of 1912, the
sullen passiveness of American Indians, of infantrymen waiting for death
at the front was part of the tremendous roar of the Marxian *Internationale.*

Hibben believed in the new world.

Here, stylistic condensation tells, particularly in the stream of consciousness and the flashback, as we flow within the mind of Hibben,
unsympathetic as one may be with those lost allegiances, those pathetic moments. Notice, then, an abrupt time transition:

Back in America
somebody got hold of a photograph of Captain Paxton Hibben laying
a wreath on Jack Reed's grave; they tried to throw him out of the
O.R.C.:

at Princeton at the twentieth reunion of his college class his class-
mates started to lynch him; they were drunk and perhaps it was just
a collegeboy prank twenty years too late but they had a noose around
his neck,

lynch the goddam red,

no more place in America for change, no more place for the old gags:
social justice, progressivism, revolt against oppression, democracy; put
the reds on the skids,

no money for them,
no jobs for them.

Then on the screen flashes the last fragment of the *Who's Who*
data Volume 15, 1928–1929:

Mem Authors League of America, Soc of Colonial Wars, Vets Foreign
Wars, Am Legion, fellow Royal and Am Geog Socs. Decorated chevalier
Order of St. Stanislas (Russian), Officer Order of the Redeemer (Greek),
Order of the Sacred Treasure (Japan). Clubs Princeton, Newspaper,
Civic (New York)

Author: Constantine and the Greek People 1920, The Famine of
Russia 1922, Henry Ward Beecher an American Portrait 1927.

d. 1929.

So ends, ironically in fadeout, the portrait of Paxton Hibben, "A
Hoosier Quixote."

Throughout a reading of the *U.S.A.* trilogy one feels the power of Dos Passos' dramatic sense, the keen antennae which he kept sensitive to the morality, speech, and physical identity of America. The cultural and individual voices fuse in our consciousness to convey moods of dissonance, danger, strain. Technically, *U.S.A.* envelops a powerful narrative continuum, in imagistic but elliptical style, constructed of strata of fact and bias. But it aesthetically creates unity while conveying a sense of disunity and disintegration. Reportorial and detached in one sense, the authorial voice nevertheless reveals a deep personal sincerity, a serious choral commitment.

We feel, as we read the portraits, the need for sympathy and identification. We feel the problems of freedom and authority in a society where sympathy and identification are too often based on false criteria. Where we find the absence of refinement, sympathy, and love we know that these elements are being called for. There is a moral sense binding the diversity and chaos together in an optative mood. We are moved to visions of wholeness by the impressions of discontinuity and inconclusiveness. Through the cacophony and journalistic clangor of discord we imagine harmony and melody.

We understand this dramatic hybrid of poetry and prose by listening. Dos Passos has listened with the ear which registers all that is precise and revealing. In reading these pieces aloud we will appreciate his genius for compressing into image and tone the essence of personality, his capacity for fluming documentary erudition into poetic substance, his skill in marshalling detail and incident for illuminative purpose and dramatic effect.

John Lydenberg

Dos Passos's *U. S. A.:*
The Words of the Hollow Men

Because James Baldwin, like Tocqueville a decade or more ago, has now become so fashionable that one cannot decently take a text from him, I shall start with Yevgeny Yevtushenko, in the hope that

Reprinted from *Essays on Determinism in American Literature,* ed. Sydney J. Krause (Kent, O.: Kent State University Press, 1964), pp. 97-107, by permission of Kent State University and the author.

he has not quite yet reached that point. In one of his poems appear the simple lines: "Let us give back to words/Their original meanings." My other non-Dos Passos text is so classic that it cannot be over-fashionable. In *A Farewell to Arms,* Gino says, "What has been done this summer cannot have been done in vain." And, as you all know, Hemingway has Frederick Henry reply: "I did not say anything. I was always embarrassed by the words sacred, glorious, and sacrifice and the expression in vain. . . . Abstract words such as glory, honor, courage, or hallow were obscene."

These quotations suggest the concern of writers with abstract words representing the ideals and values of their society. Both Yevtushenko and Hemingway say that these words have lost their glory, their true meaning. But they take diametrically opposed attitudes toward the role the words will play in their writings. Representing the party of Hope, Yevtushenko is the social and political idealist, the reformer, the artist who sees his art as a weapon in man's unceasing struggle for a better world. Representing the party of Despair, Hemingway abjures political concerns, makes his separate peace, and develops an art unconcerned with social ideals. Thus they symbolize two extremes: writers at one pole—Yevtushenko's—will utilize the words, will insist on doing so; writers at the other—Hemingway's—will dispense with them altogether, or try to do so, as did Hemingway in most of his early fiction.

Dos Passos falls between the extremes, but instead of presenting us with a golden mean he gives something more like an unstable compound of the two. Hemingway abandons the words because he can see no relation between them and the realities, and creates a world stripped of the values represented by the words. By contrast, reformers—who are equally insistent on the disparity between the ideals and the realities—are unwilling to reject the words and strive, like Yevtushenko, to give back to them their original meanings. Dos Passos can neither abandon nor revivify the words. Like Hemingway he feels that they have been made obscene and he can find no way in his art to redeem them. Yet like any reformer he puts them at the center of his work.

Critics have often held that the protagonist of *U.S.A.* is society. I could almost maintain that it is, instead, "the words." Dos Passos seems obsessed by them: he cares about them passionately and cannot abandon them, but at the same time he is made sick at heart—nay at stomach—by the way they have been spoiled. So he concerns himself with problems of social values, ever returning to the words, "as a dog to his vomit" (to use the inelegant but expressive Biblical phrase). *U.S.A.* tastes sour because the words are tainted and indigestible, but neither here nor in his other fiction can Dos Passos spew them forth once and for all as could the Hemingways of our literature.

In two well-known passages, Dos Passos makes explicit his feeling about the words. These—the most eloquent and deeply felt parts of *U.S.A.*—are the Camera Eyes focused on the execution of Sacco and Vanzetti. In the first, immediately preceding the Mary French section on the last desperate days before the executions, he asks:

> how make them feel who are your oppressors America
> rebuild the ruined words worn slimy in the mouths of lawyers district-attorneys collegepresidents judges without the old words the immigrants haters of oppression brought to Plymouth how can you know who are your betrayers America . . . ? (*Big Money,* 437)

In the second, after the execution, he says:

> we the beaten crowd together . . . sit hunched with bowed heads on benches and hear the old words of the haters of oppression made new in sweat and agony tonight
> our work is over the scribbled phrases the nights typing releases the smell of the printshop the sharp reek of newprinted leaflets the rush for Western Union stringing words into wires the search for stinging words to make you feel who are your oppressors America
> America our nation has been beaten by strangers who have turned our language inside out who have taken the clean words our fathers spoke and made them slimy and foul (462)*

Just as Dos Passos makes the Sacco-Vanzetti affair symbolic of his vision of the state of the nation, so, in talking about the "old words," "the clean words our fathers spoke," and "the old American speech," he is alluding to his ideals, to the American dream, and in describing the words now as "ruined," "slimy and foul," and "turned . . . inside out," he is expressing his sense of the betrayal of the dream.

"Mostly *U.S.A.* is the speech of the people," says Dos Passos to conclude the prose poem he added as preface to the trilogy. Maybe. But *U.S.A.*, the novel, in no way carries out that Sandburg-like suggestion of faith in the people and delight in their talk. It contains none of the salty talk, the boastful talk, the folksy talk, the "wise"

---

*Page references documenting the quotations from *U.S.A.* are to the Modern Library edition (1937); those for *First Encounter* (originally published as *One Man's Initiation*) are to the New York, 1945, edition.

talk that is the staple of much "realistic" American fiction. Actually, we discover, on re-examination of these novels, that dialogue plays a smaller role than we might have thought it did. What little talk there is is either purely functional, merely a way of getting on with the narrative: "Shall we go to bed?" "Where can I get a drink?" "God I feel lousy this morning." Or it is banal and stereotyped. Whenever his characters express anything resembling ideas they talk only in tired slogans; the words have been drained of meaning, and the characters mouthing them are empty puppets.

Here is one example. I would give many more, had I time, for the real effect is gained only through the continuous repetition of the vaporous phrases. This is from *1919*, the novel written during the time Dos Passos was presumably most favorably inclined toward Marxism and the Communists. One might have expected that here if anywhere the words of a communist, Don Stevens in this instance, would carry some conviction. Instead Dos Passos makes them sound mechanical, false, flat, like counterfeit coins. The effect is heightened here, as in many other places, by giving us the words in indirect dialog.

> He said that there wasn't a chinaman's chance that the U.S. would keep out of the war; the Germans were winning, the working class all over Europe was on the edge of revolt, the revolution in Russia was the beginning of the worldwide social revolution and the bankers knew it and Wilson knew it; the only question was whether the industrial workers in the east and the farmers and casual laborers in the middle west and west would stand for war. The entire press was bought and muzzled. The Morgans had to fight or go bankrupt. "It's the greatest conspiracy in history." (131)

This is the way the words sound in passage after passage. The ruined words dribble from the mouths of Dos Passos' hollow men. Within is nothing but clichés, phrases having no meaning for the speaker and conveying none to the listener. *This* is the speech of the people in Dos Passos's *U.S.A.*, and it does much to establish the tone of the whole trilogy.

But if the words are often empty and meaningless, they often too have a very real meaning, vicious and perverted. The old words of the American dream have been "turned . . . inside out"; now they are the lies by which the new Americans live. The theme of the transformation of the clean words into lies had been baldly stated in Dos Passos's first novel, *One Man's Initiation*. Early in the book, Martin Howe dreams romantically of his mission as the ocean steamer carries him "over there": "And very faintly, like music heard across the water in the evening, blurred into strange harmonies, his old watchwords echo a little in his mind. Like the red flame of the sunset setting fire to opal sea and sky, the old exaltation, the old flame that would consume to ashes all the lies in the world, the trumpet-blast under which the walls of Jericho would fall down, stirs and broods in the womb of his grey lassitude" (14). Then as Martin is first going up to the front, he comes to adopt a new conception in which the lies are all-inclusive, his "old watchwords" now no different from the rest of the world's lies. A stranger appears and explains it to him: "Think, man, think of all the oceans of lies through all the ages that must have been necessary to make this possible! Think of this new particular vintage of lies that has been so industriously pumped out of the press and the pulpit. . . . The lies are like a sticky juice over-spreading the world, a living, growing flypaper to catch and gum the wings of every human soul" (30). Finally, Martin talks in much the same way himself: " 'What terrifies me . . . is their power to enslave our minds. . . . America, as you know, is ruled by the press. . . . People seem to so love to be fooled. . . . We are slaves of bought intellect, willing slaves' " (144). And a French anarchist takes up the theme and makes the moral explicit: " 'Oh, but we are all such dupes. . . . First we must fight the lies. It is the lies that choke us' " (156).

In *U.S.A.*, Dos Passos does not *tell* us about the lies, he makes us feel them. The Newsreels are his most obvious device for showing us the "sticky juice" of lies in which Americans are caught. The opening lines of *The 42nd Parallel* are: "It was that emancipated race/That was chargin up the hill;/Up to where them insurrectos/Was afightin fit to kill." This hill is not San Juan but a hill in the Philippines. And that first Newsreel ends with Senator Beveridge's lucid bluster: "The twentieth century will be American. American thought will dominate it. American progress will give it color and direction. American deeds will make it illustrious. . . . The regeneration of the world, physical as well as moral, has begun, and revolutions never move backwards" (5).

One recognizable pattern keeps recurring in the shifting kaleidoscope of the Newsreels: that is—the official lies disguised as popular truths. We see—and hear—the rhetoric of the American Way drummed into the heads of the American public, by advertisements, newspaper headlines, newspaper stories, politicians' statements, businessmen's statements. In contrast to these standardized verbalizations about happy, prosperous, good America, the Newsreels give continual flashes of Dos Passos's "real" America—of fads and follies, hardships and horrors. More striking even than the contrasts within these collages are those between the shimmering surface of the Newsreels and the sardonic realities of the Portraits, and above all the dreary lives of his fictional characters.

The narratives of these lives take up the greater part of the book, of course, and our reaction to it depends to a great extent on our evaluation of the characters. My suggestion is that it is by their use of "the words" that we judge them. And here, *mirabile dictu,* we come at last to the theme of "determinism."

That *U.S.A.* is strongly naturalistic and deterministic is obvious to all. Readers who judge it a major work of fiction do so in part because of its success in portraying characters as helpless individuals caught in a world they have not made and cannot control. Less admiring critics are apt to consider its weakness to be the weakness of the characters, sometimes even implying that Dos Passos's failure to create free, responsible heroes was a failure of execution. Whatever their assessment of the novel, all agree that *U.S.A.* is starkly deterministic. None of its characters has free will, none determines his fate, all move like automatons.

The chief way in which Dos Passos makes us feel that his characters—or non-characters—are determined is by showing their choices to be decisions. They simply are doing so and so, and continue thus until they find themselves, or we find them, doing something else.

Here are two examples. The first, a long one, includes two decisions, one a reversal of the other. Note here—for future reference—what the protagonist, Richard Ellsworth Savage, does with the words, and note also how the indirect dialogue accentuates the feeling of cliché and slogan. Dick is "deciding" what he should do about the war and about his college education.

In the Easter vacation, after the Armed Ship Bill had passed Dick had a long talk with Mr. Cooper who wanted to get him a job in Washington, because he said a boy of his talent oughtn't to endanger his career by joining the army and already there was talk of conscription. Dick blushed becomingly and said he felt it would be against his conscience to help in the war in any way. They talked a long time without getting anywhere about duty to the state and party leadership and highest expediency. In the end Mr. Cooper made him promise not to take any rash step without consulting him. [Note that Dick has now "decided" that his "principles" forbid him to enter any war work.] Back in Cambridge everybody was drilling and going to lectures on military science. Dick was finishing up the four year course in three years and had to work hard, but nothing in the courses seemed to mean anything any more. He managed to find time to polish up a group of sonnets called Morituri Te Salutant that he sent to a prize competition run by *The Literary Digest*. It won the prize but the editors wrote back that they would prefer a note of hope in the last sestet. Dick put in the note of hope [so go the words!] and sent the hundred dollars to Mother to go to Atlantic City with. He discovered that if he went into war work he could get his degree that spring without taking any exams and went in to Boston one day without saying anything to anybody and signed up in the volunteer ambulance service. [Now he has "decided" that his "principles" no longer prevent him from war work.] (*1919*, 95–96)

And here is the sound of a Dos Passos character "deciding" to have an abortion:

Of course she could have the baby if she wanted to [Don Stevens said] it would spoil her usefulness in the struggle for several months and he didn't think this was the time for it. It was the first time they'd quarreled. She said he was heartless. He said they had to sacrifice their personal feelings for the working class, and stormed out of the house in a temper. In the end she had an abortion but she had to write her mother again for money to pay for it. (*Big Money*, 447)

These examples of important decisions presented as simply something that the character happened somehow to do are not exceptional; they are typical. I think I can say safely that there are *no* decisions in the three novels that are presented in a significantly different way.

To this extent, then, *U.S.A.* is systematically, rigidly, effectively deterministic. But there is a fault in its rigid structure, a softness in its determinism, and—in opposition to both the friendly and unfriendly critics of Dos Passos—I would suggest that a large part of the book's success comes precisely from the author's failure to be as consistently deterministic as he thinks he wants to be. True as it is that we never identify with any of his characters as we do with conventionally free characters, it is equally true that we do not regard them all with the nice objectivity required by the deterministic logic. Some we consider "good" and some "bad," just as though they were in fact responsible human beings making free choices. And these judgments that we make, however illogically, we base largely upon the way in which the different characters treat those crucial abstract words.

Some characters are essentially neutral—or perhaps I should say that we feel them to be truly determined. We look upon Margo

Dowling, Eveline Hutchins, Eleanor Stoddard, and Charley Anderson with a coolly detached eye, even though we may feel that in their various ways the women are somewhat bitchy. And although Daughter, and Joe and Janey Williams tend to arouse our sympathies, we view them quite dispassionately. Certainly we do not consider any of these as responsible moral agents. And none of them shows any inclination to be concerned with the words.

In contrast to the neutral characters are Mac, Ben Compton, and Mary French. Dos Passos likes them and makes us like them because they affirm the values which he holds and wishes his readers to accept. Each of them uses the words, tries to uphold the true meaning of the "old words," and fights to rebuild the ruined words. Although their decisions are described in the same way that all other decisions are, we feel that their choices of the words are deliberate, and are acts of freedom for which they take the responsibility. Mac leaves his girl in San Francisco to go to Goldfield as a printer for the Wobblies because he finds that his life is meaningless when he is not using and acting out the words. Later, after his marriage, he escapes again from the bourgeois trap because he can't bear not to be talking with his old comrades about their dream and ideals. Finally, unable to do anything but talk and unable to find a way to make the old words new or effective, he sinks back into the conventional rut of the other unfree characters. Ben Compton insists on talking peace and socialism after the United States has entered the war, freely choosing thereby to be taken by the police and imprisoned. During the war, it seems, the old words may not be used in public until they have been converted into the official lies.

Mary French is generally considered Dos Passos's most sympathetic character in *U.S.A.* She is certainly associated with the words throughout, and in her work with the 1919 steel strikers and the Sacco-Vanzetti committee she is actively engaged in the attempt to "renew" the words and make them effective in the fight for justice. But, significantly, she does not employ them much. Not only have they been worn slimy in the mouths of her enemies, but they are continually being perverted by her co-workers and supposed friends, the ostensible renovators of the words. So, in the final section of *The Big Money,* we find her collecting clothes for the struck coal miners, doing good, but not a good that goes beyond the mere maintenance of brute existence. Anything of more significance would demand use of the words, and at this point in his writing, the words, to Dos Passos, have been ruined beyond redemption.

And then there are the bad guys, J. Ward Moorehouse and Richard Ellsworth Savage. They are as hollow as any other Dos Passos men, their decisions, like all others, non-decisions. But where Joe and Janey Williams make us sad, these make us mad. We dislike them and blame them, just as though they had really chosen.

Dos Passos makes us feel that a character is responsible for the words he chooses. To explain just *how* Dos Passos does that is not easy, but I think it goes, in part, something like this. We don't blame Dick for drinking too much or for wenching, any more than we blame Charley Anderson or Joe Williams. These activities seem to be instinctive reactions, self-defeating but natural escapes from freedom. Part of the reason we feel Dick and the others determined in their dissipation, and consequently do not blame them, is because the characters blame themselves, regret what they do and feebly resolve not to do it again. Thus when they fall back into their old, familiar ways, we feel that they are doing what they do not want to do, do not will to do. But when we come to another sort of action, the choice of words, no character is shown regretting the abstract words he uses. Thus the character implicitly approves his choice of words, he seems to be acting freely, and we tend to hold him responsible.

To get back to our bad guys, Moorehouse and Savage are the successful exploiters in the trilogy, and on first thought we might assume that fact would suffice to make them culpable. But they are not the usual exploiters found in proletarian novels: big bad businessmen gouging the workers, manufacturers grinding the faces of the poor. Indeed they don't seem to hurt anyone. They exploit not people but words, or people, impersonally, by means of the words. Their profession is "public relations." (We might look at them as precursors of the Madison Avenue villains of post World War II fiction, and infinitely superior ones, at that.) Their job is to persuade people to buy a product or to act in a particular way. Their means of persuasion is words. And the words they use are to a great extent "the words," the words of the American dream. They talk cooperation, justice, opportunity, freedom, equality.

Here are two brief quotations from J. Ward Moorehouse. He and Savage are preparing a publicity campaign for old Doc Bingham's patent medicines—now called "proprietary" medicines. (You will remember that Doc was Mac's first employer at the beginning of the trilogy, as owner-manager of "The Truthseeker Literary Distributing Co., Inc.") The first quotation is part of J. W.'s argument to a complaisant senator: "But, senator, . . . it's the principle of the thing. Once government interference in business is established as a precedent it means the end of liberty and private initiative in this country. . . . What this bill purports to do is to take the right of selfmedication from the American people" (505-506). And in this next one he is talking to his partner Savage about the advertising—no, publicity—campaign: "Of course self-service, independence, individualism is the word I gave the boys in the beginning. This is going to be more than a publicity campaign, it's going to be a campaign for Americanism" (494).

Here at last we have arrived at the source—or at least one major source—of the cancerous evil that swells malignantly through the books. Here we observe the manufacturers of the all-pervasive lies busily at work, here we see the words being deliberately perverted. And we cannot consider the perverters of the words as merely helpless automatons or innocents; they deliberately choose their words and we judge them as villains.

So, in conclusion, Dos Passos finds that the old words of the immigrant haters of oppression, which should have set Americans free, have instead been worn slimy in their mouths. And these words are in effect central actors in *U.S.A.* They determine our attitudes toward the characters who use and misuse them, establish the tone of hollow futility that rings throughout the trilogy, and leave in our mouths the bitter after-taste of nausea. The novels that followed, to make the *District of Columbia* trilogy, emphasize Dos Passos's sick obsession with these words. In the first, the humanitarian socialist dream comes to us in the clichés and jargon of American communists; in the second, the American dream is conveyed to us through the demagogery of a vulgar Louisiana dictator; in the third the dream of New Deal reform has been turned into a nightmare by cynical opportunists and time-serving bureaucrats who exploit the old words anew.

No longer able to imagine a way of giving to words their original meanings, after *U.S.A.,* Dos Passos could still not abandon them for some more palatable subject. And so he seemed to take the worst part of the worlds of Yevtushenko and Hemingway. But in *U.S.A.* he could still write about Mac and Ben Compton and Mary French; he could still feel some hope that the ruined words might be rebuilt; he could still imagine the dream to be yet a possibility. In *U.S.A.* his despair was not yet total and his dual vision of the words brought to these novels a tension, a vitality, and a creative energy he would never be able to muster again.